The Bright Blue Thinking Book

Book 2

by Lori Mammen

a focus on family learning

Published by

ECS Learning Systems, Inc.

About the Author

Lori Mammen, a professional educator for more than 20 years, is a graduate of The Ohio State University in Columbus, Ohio. She is the co-creator and editor of *Writing Teacher*™ and *THINK*™ magazines, and works with teachers and students in the areas of writing, reading, and thinking skills.

Lori lives with her husband Sam and children Sarah, Suzanne, and Christopher in Bulverde, Texas.

Published by
ECS Learning Systems, Inc.
P.O. Box 791437
San Antonio, Texas 78279-1437

ISBN 1-57022-111-1

© Copyright 1997 by ECS Learning Systems, Inc., San Antonio, Texas. All rights reserved. No part of this publication may be reproduced, stored in a retrieval system, or transmitted in any way or by any means (electronic, mechanical, photocopying, recording, or otherwise) without prior written permission from ECS Learning Systems, Inc., with the following exception. Photocopying of student worksheets by a teacher who purchased this publication for his/her own class is permissible. Reproduction of any part of this publication for an entire school or for a school system or for commercial sale is strictly prohibited.

Printed in the United States of America.

Home Study Collection™ is a trademark of ECS Learning Systems, Inc.

Editor: Shirley J. Durst, Graphic Artist: Kathleen Magargee. Art on pages 65, 79, 96, 98 by Corel GALLERY.

Home Study Collection™ books are available at special discounts for bulk purchases by corporations, institutions, and other organizations. For more information, please contact the Special Sales Department, ECS Learning Systems, Inc., P. O. Box 791437, San Antonio, Texas 78279-1437, 1-800-688-3224.

Think About It

If the ocean could speak, what would it say? How many green, shiny things can you list in three minutes? Would you rather have a pet dragon or a pet gorilla?

If you think questions like this are fun to answer, then *The Bright Blue Thinking Book* is for you! It's filled with lots of ideas to spark your thinking.

This is **your** book. Start wherever you like. Finish everything, or do just the parts you like best. Fit all your ideas on the pages, or let them spill onto other paper. It's all up to you.

The Bright Blue Thinking Book goes almost anywhere. Use it during long car trips or vacations. Choose an idea-starter for a school assignment, or use one for your journal or diary. *The Bright Blue Thinking Book* is even great family fun.

So, turn on your thinking machine. On your mark, get set...**THINK!**

© ECS Learning Systems, Inc. All Rights Reserved.

Write the words for a song about sunshine. Use the tune to "Three Blind Mice."

© ECS Learning Systems, Inc. All Rights Reserved.

Create an exciting picture with exclamation points.

© ECS Learning Systems, Inc. All Rights Reserved.

!

Sleeping is like ______________________ because...

3–minute list—

Household items that are about six inches long...

Go!

_______________ _______________ _______________

_______________ _______________ _______________

_______________ _______________ _______________

_______________ _______________ _______________

_______________ _______________ _______________

Inch is to foot as _______________ is to _______________ .

© ECS Learning Systems, Inc. All Rights Reserved.

When I hear the word ***city****, I think about—*

Draw!

© ECS Learning Systems, Inc.   All Rights Reserved.

Choose—Would you rather be

a desert

or

a rain forest?

Why?

____

____

____

Desert is to ____________________ as rain forest is to ____________________ .

© ECS Learning Systems, Inc. All Rights Reserved.

You have a marble, a straw, and white paper. Invent a new game.

© ECS Learning Systems, Inc. All Rights Reserved.

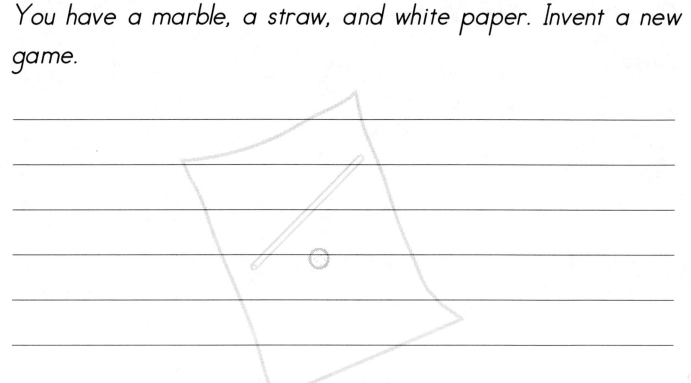

Good citizens should always—

Draw!

© ECS Learning Systems, Inc. All Rights Reserved.

Citizen is to nation as ______________________ is to ______________________ .

Good citizens should never—

Draw!

© ECS Learning Systems, Inc. All Rights Reserved.

The answer is ***electricity****. What are some questions?*

1. ____?

2. ____?

3. ____?

4. ____?

5. ____?

© ECS Learning Systems, Inc. All Rights Reserved.

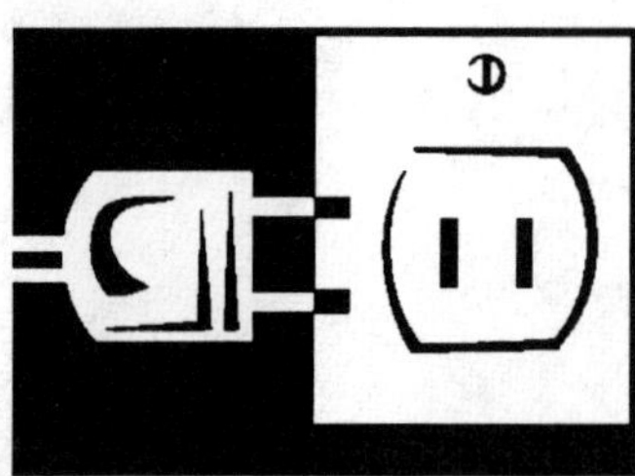

What I Like To Do

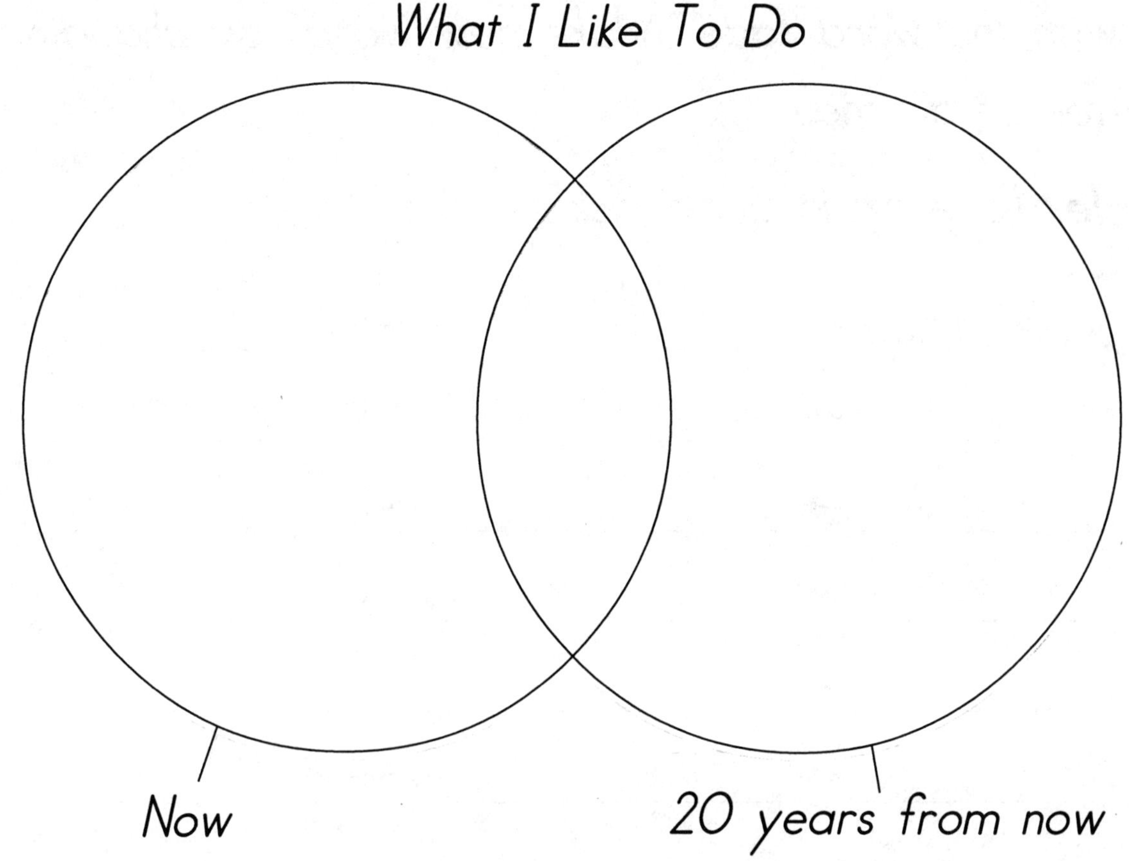

© ECS Learning Systems, Inc. All Rights Reserved.

Start with the word **face**. Make new words by changing one letter at a time.

Example: face → lace → lack

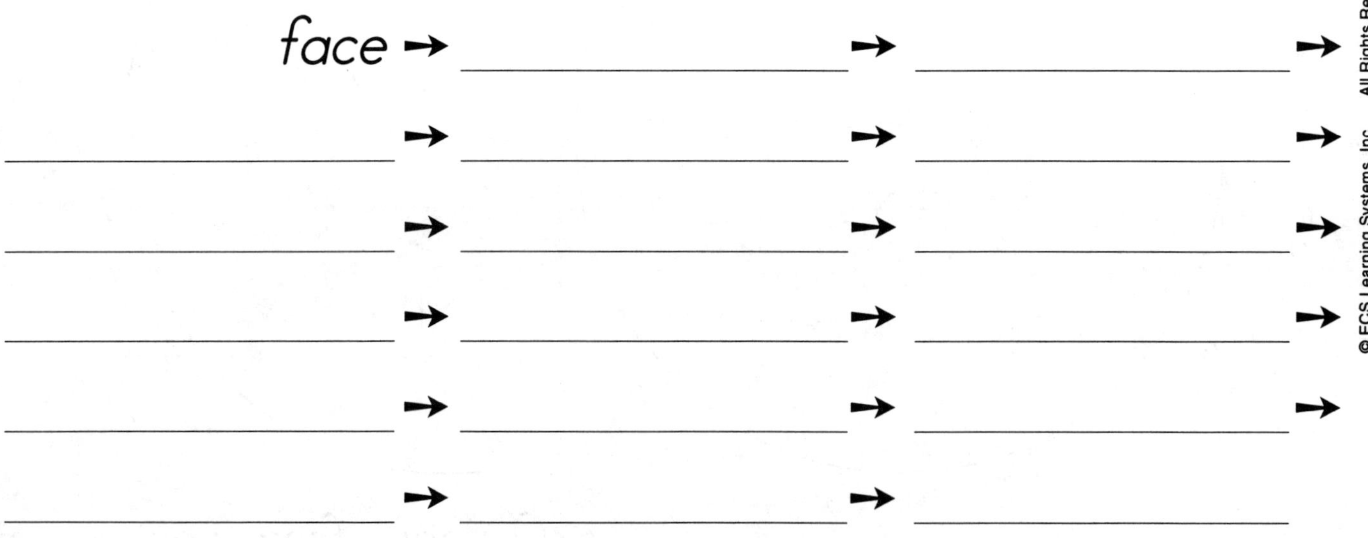

© ECS Learning Systems, Inc. All Rights Reserved.

Show 1/2 in three different ways.

© ECS Learning Systems, Inc. All Rights Reserved.

Half is to whole as ______________________ is to ______________________ .

Design a new symbol for the U.S.A.

© ECS Learning Systems, Inc. All Rights Reserved.

A flag is like ______________________ because...

Create a t–shirt message about the environment.

© ECS Learning Systems, Inc. All Rights Reserved.

Trace the shape of your state. Add lines to make an animal picture.

© ECS Learning Systems, Inc. All Rights Reserved.

State is to country as ____________________ is to ____________________ .

If the ocean could speak, what would it say?

© ECS Learning Systems, Inc. All Rights Reserved.

How would you answer?

3-minute list—

Seeds that people can eat...

Go!

______	______	______
______	______	______
______	______	______
______	______	______
______	______	______

Seed is to plant as ______________ is to ______________ .

© ECS Learning Systems, Inc. All Rights Reserved.

If anger were a shape, what shape would it be?

Draw!

© ECS Learning Systems, Inc. All Rights Reserved.

Cities of the future will probably...

A skyscraper is like ______________________ because...

© ECS Learning Systems, Inc. All Rights Reserved.

If people had three hands instead of two...

© ECS Learning Systems, Inc. All Rights Reserved.

The President has a cold. Create a get-well card.

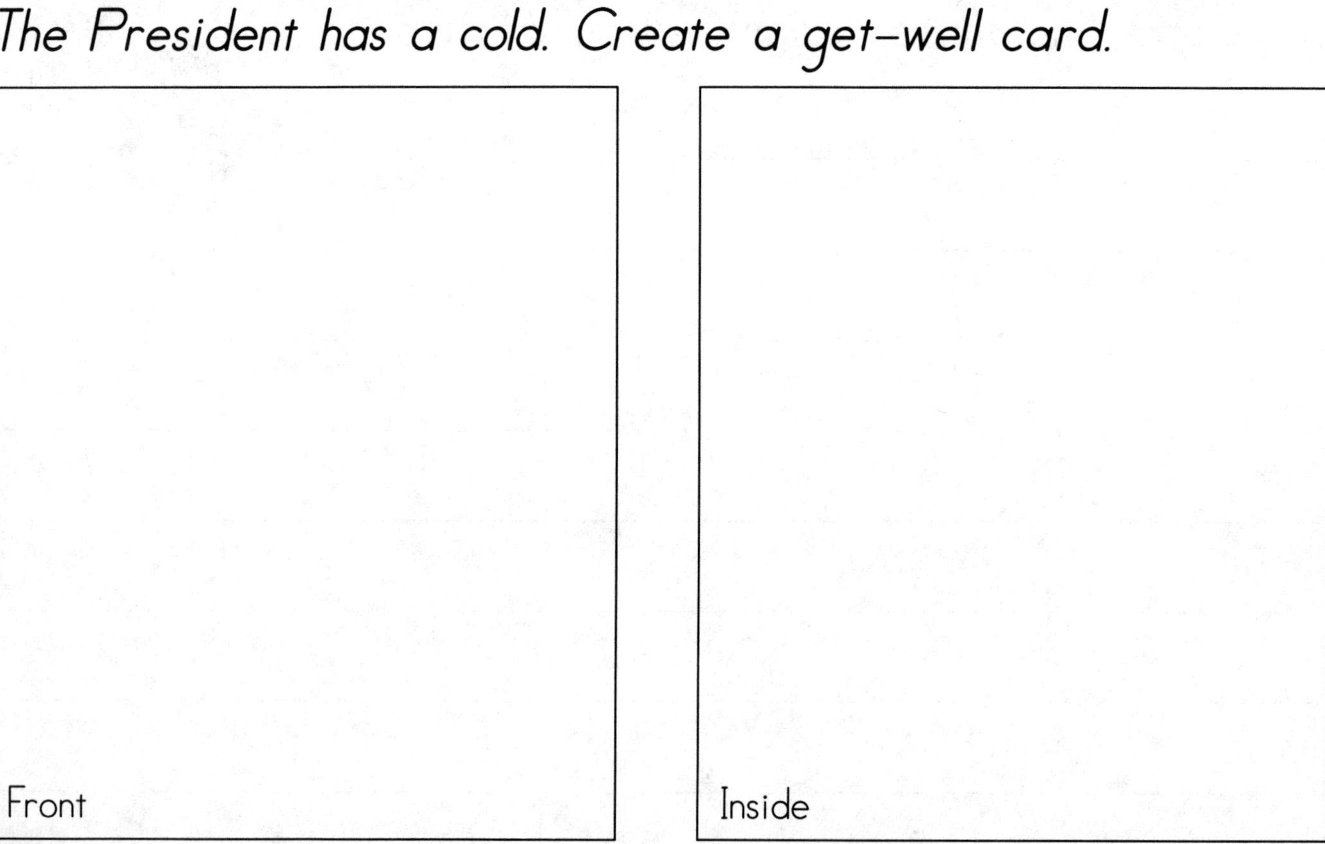

© ECS Learning Systems, Inc. All Rights Reserved.

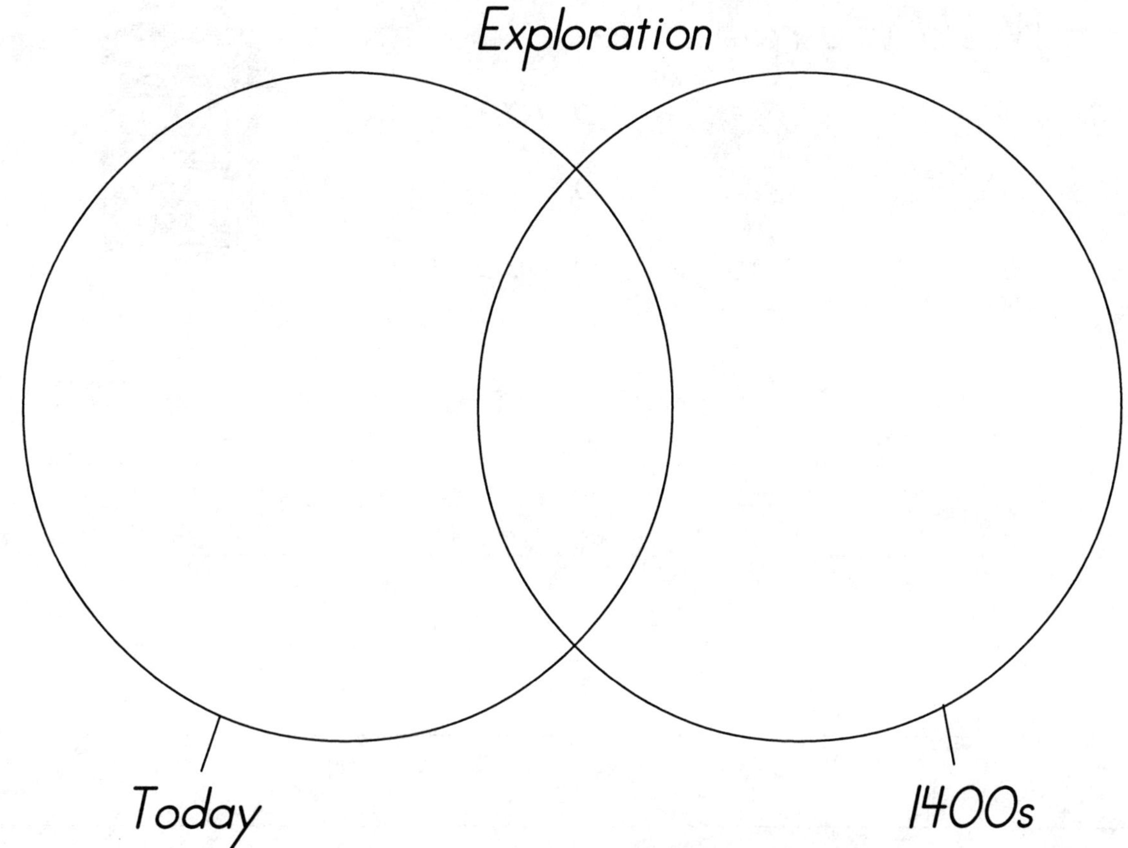

© ECS Learning Systems, Inc. All Rights Reserved.

Choose—Would you rather be

a fan

or

a heater?

Why?

____

____

____

____

____

© ECS Learning Systems, Inc. All Rights Reserved.

3–minute list—

Foods that grow underground...

Go!

______________ ______________ ______________

______________ ______________ ______________

______________ ______________ ______________

______________ ______________ ______________

______________ ______________ ______________

Under is to ______________ as over is to ______________ .

© ECS Learning Systems, Inc. All Rights Reserved.

Quiet sounds...

Shhhh!

Quiet is to ______________________ as loud is to ______________________ .

© ECS Learning Systems, Inc. All Rights Reserved.

Quiet colors...

Shhhh!

© ECS Learning Systems, Inc. All Rights Reserved.

My favorite quiet color...

Start with the word **mare**. Make new words by changing one letter at a time.

Example: mare ➔ mate ➔ late

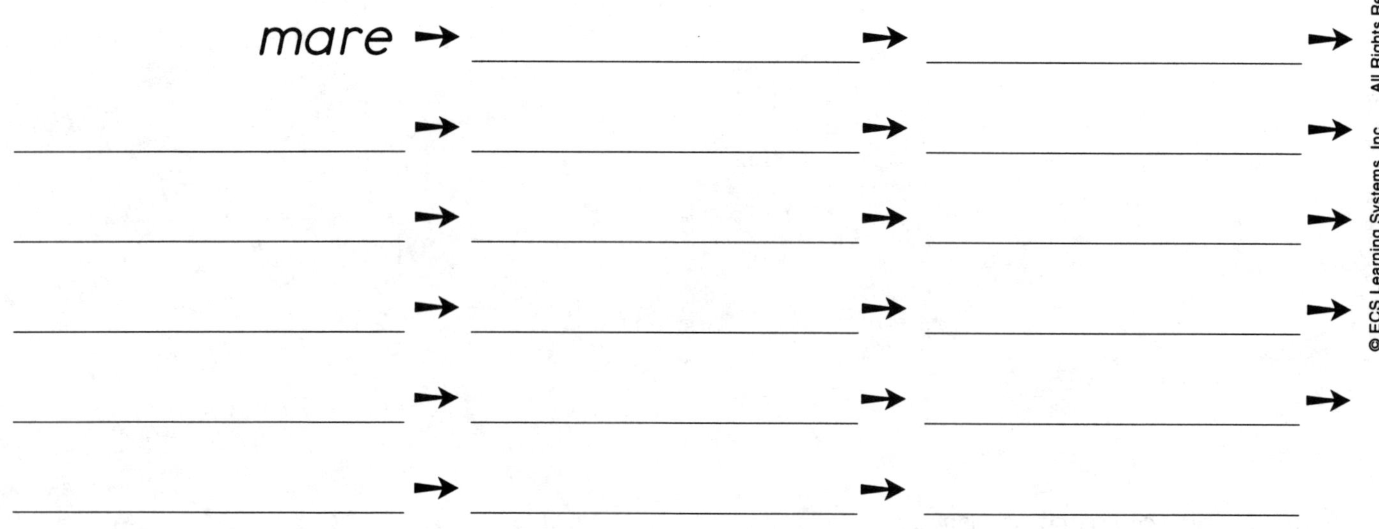

© ECS Learning Systems, Inc. All Rights Reserved.

*When I hear the word **forest**, I think about—*

Branch is to tree as ______________________ is to ______________________ .

© ECS Learning Systems, Inc. All Rights Reserved.

You must lift a ***heavy*** *box. How will you make the job easier?*

Draw!

Lift is to ____________________ as push is to ____________________ .

© ECS Learning Systems, Inc. All Rights Reserved.

List numbers with digits that have a product of 20.

Example: *451; 4 x 5 x 1 = 20*

© ECS Learning Systems, Inc. All Rights Reserved.

If happiness were a color, what color would it be?

Why?

© ECS Learning Systems, Inc. All Rights Reserved.

3–minute list—

Ways people show courage...

Go!

___________________ ___________________ ___________________

___________________ ___________________ ___________________

___________________ ___________________ ___________________

___________________ ___________________ ___________________

___________________ ___________________ ___________________

Courage is like ________________________ because...

© ECS Learning Systems, Inc. All Rights Reserved.

Write the words to a song about a butterfly's life. Use the tune for "Happy Birthday."

____

____

____

____

____

____

Butterfly is to ____________________ as moth is to ____________________ .

© ECS Learning Systems, Inc. All Rights Reserved.

You are looking through a microscope. Suddenly you see...

Draw!

© ECS Learning Systems, Inc. All Rights Reserved.

Things in the Kitchen

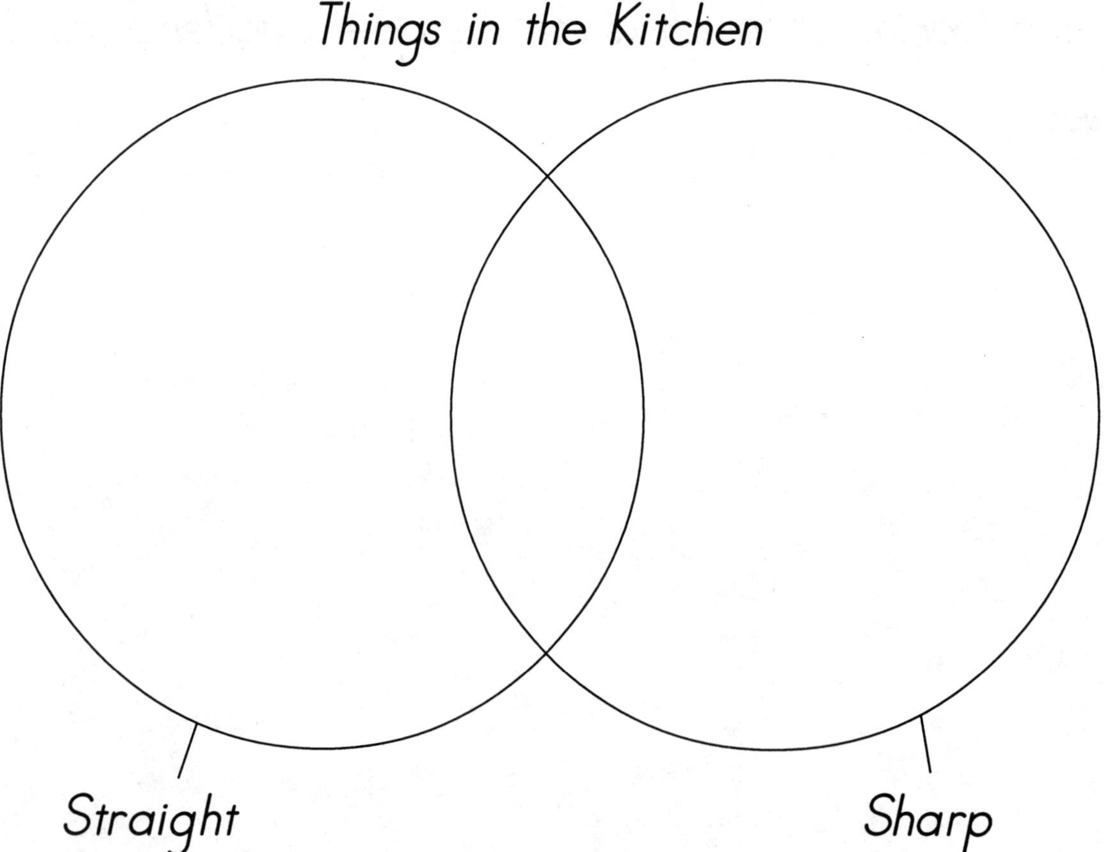

© ECS Learning Systems, Inc. All Rights Reserved.

The newspaper ran the story of Goldilocks and the Three Bears. Write the headline.

A headline is like ______________________ because...

© ECS Learning Systems, Inc. All Rights Reserved.

Choose—Would you rather be

peanut butter

or

jelly?

Why?

© ECS Learning Systems, Inc. All Rights Reserved.

The answer is **72**. Write some problems.

☐ + ☐ = 72

☐ − ☐ = 72

☐ x ☐ = 72

☐ ÷ ☐ = 72

72 is to 9 as ______________ is to ______________ .

© ECS Learning Systems, Inc. All Rights Reserved.

You have a pencil, string, and a paper clip. Create a toy.

Draw!

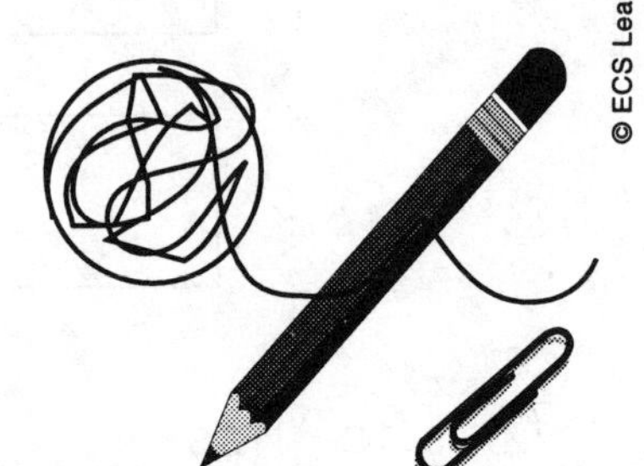

© ECS Learning Systems, Inc. All Rights Reserved.

3-minute list—

Things that are both green and shiny...

Go!

_______________ _______________ _______________

_______________ _______________ _______________

_______________ _______________ _______________

_______________ _______________ _______________

_______________ _______________ _______________

My favorite green and shiny thing is _______________ because...

© ECS Learning Systems, Inc. All Rights Reserved.

Write a tongue twister about your favorite animal.

© ECS Learning Systems, Inc. All Rights Reserved.

Use the zigzag as part of a party picture.

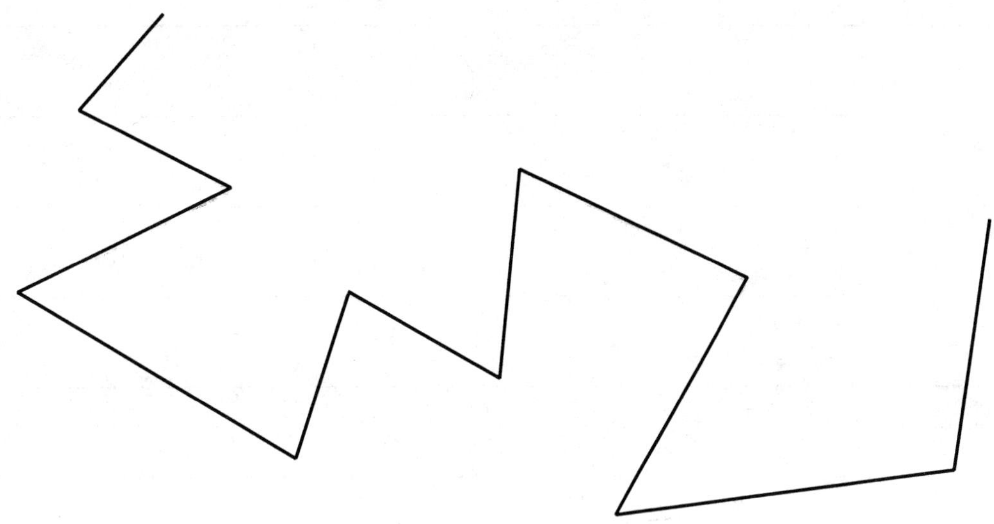

Zigzag is to line as ______________________ is to ______________________ .

© ECS Learning Systems, Inc. All Rights Reserved.

Late at night, the wind sounds...

© ECS Learning Systems, Inc.   All Rights Reserved.

List—10 ways to know when you've really goofed.

A mistake is like ____________________ because...

© ECS Learning Systems, Inc. All Rights Reserved.

When I hear the word ***celebrate****, I think about—*

Draw!

Celebrate is to party as ______________________ is to ______________________ .

© ECS Learning Systems, Inc. All Rights Reserved.

If I were a seed, I would want...

© ECS Learning Systems, Inc. All Rights Reserved.

Write the words to a song about math. Use the tune to "Mary Had a Little Lamb."

© ECS Learning Systems, Inc. All Rights Reserved.

Choose—Would you rather be

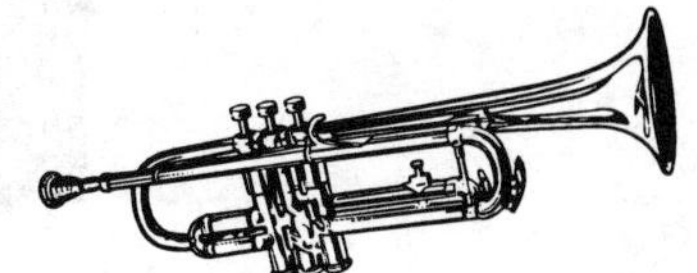

a tuba

or

a trumpet?

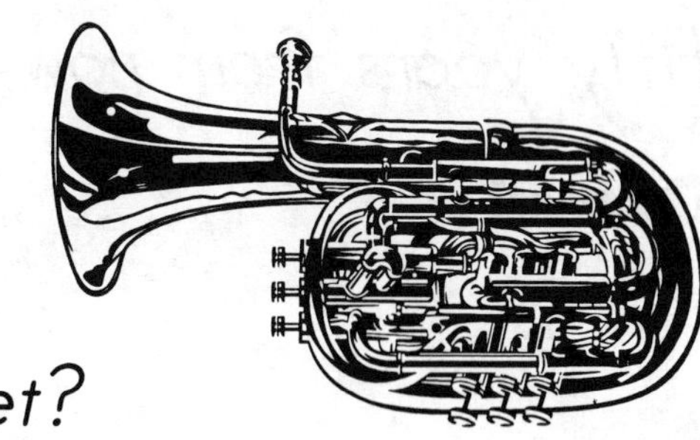

Why?

© ECS Learning Systems, Inc. All Rights Reserved.

Fifty years from now schools will be—

Draw!

Student is to ______________________ as teacher is to ______________________ .

© ECS Learning Systems, Inc. All Rights Reserved.

The answer is ***Australia***. *What are the questions?*

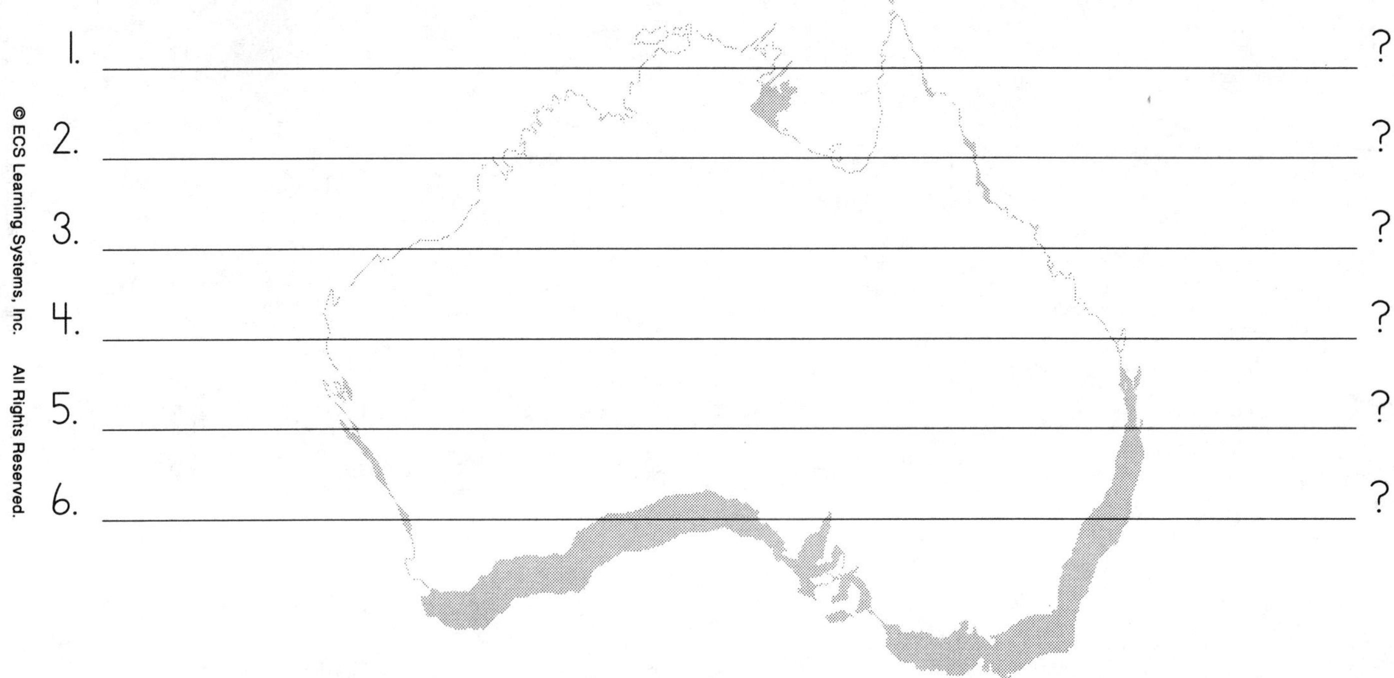

1. ____?
2. ____?
3. ____?
4. ____?
5. ____?
6. ____?

© ECS Learning Systems, Inc. All Rights Reserved.

List 6 ways to make a better chair.

1. ______________________________

2. ______________________________

3. ______________________________

4. ______________________________

5. ______________________________

6. ______________________________

© ECS Learning Systems, Inc. All Rights Reserved.

Draw a picture of a "better chair."

Chair is to sit as ______________________ is to ______________________ .

© ECS Learning Systems, Inc. All Rights Reserved.

*The **tele** in telescope means far away. How many **tele** words can you list?*

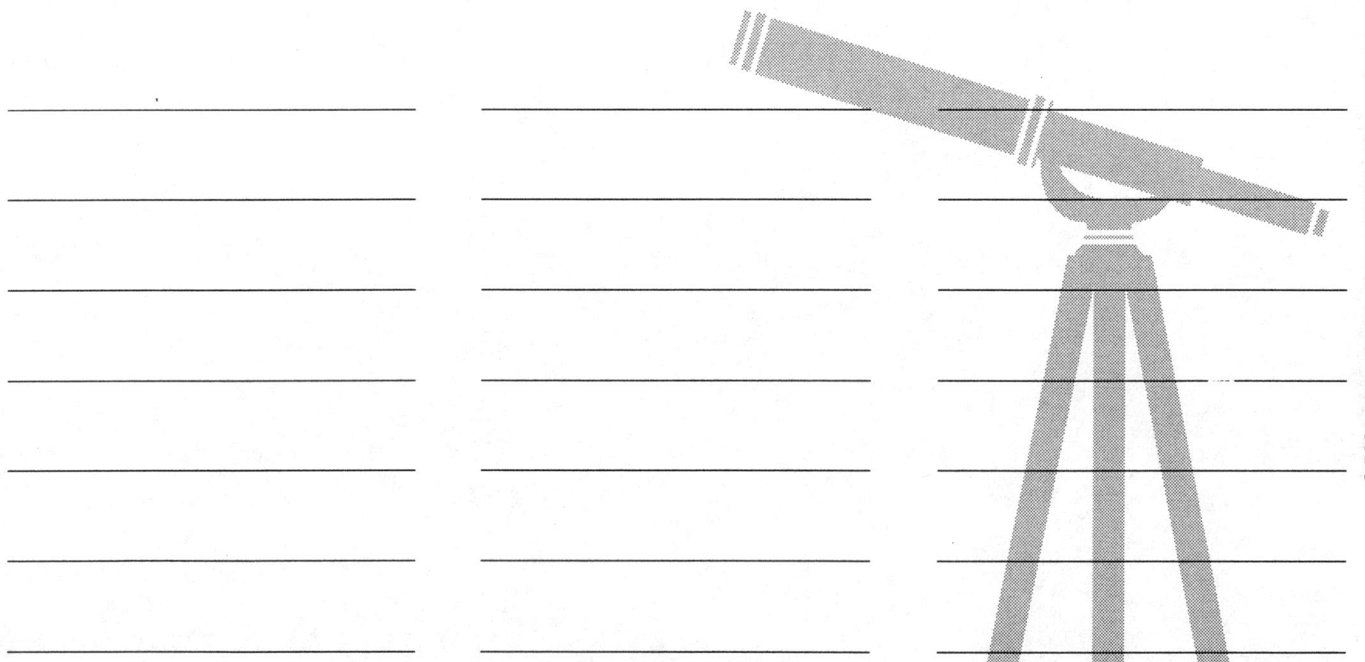

© ECS Learning Systems, Inc. All Rights Reserved.

Look at the character. What is he thinking?

© ECS Learning Systems, Inc. All Rights Reserved.

Thinking is like ______________________ because...

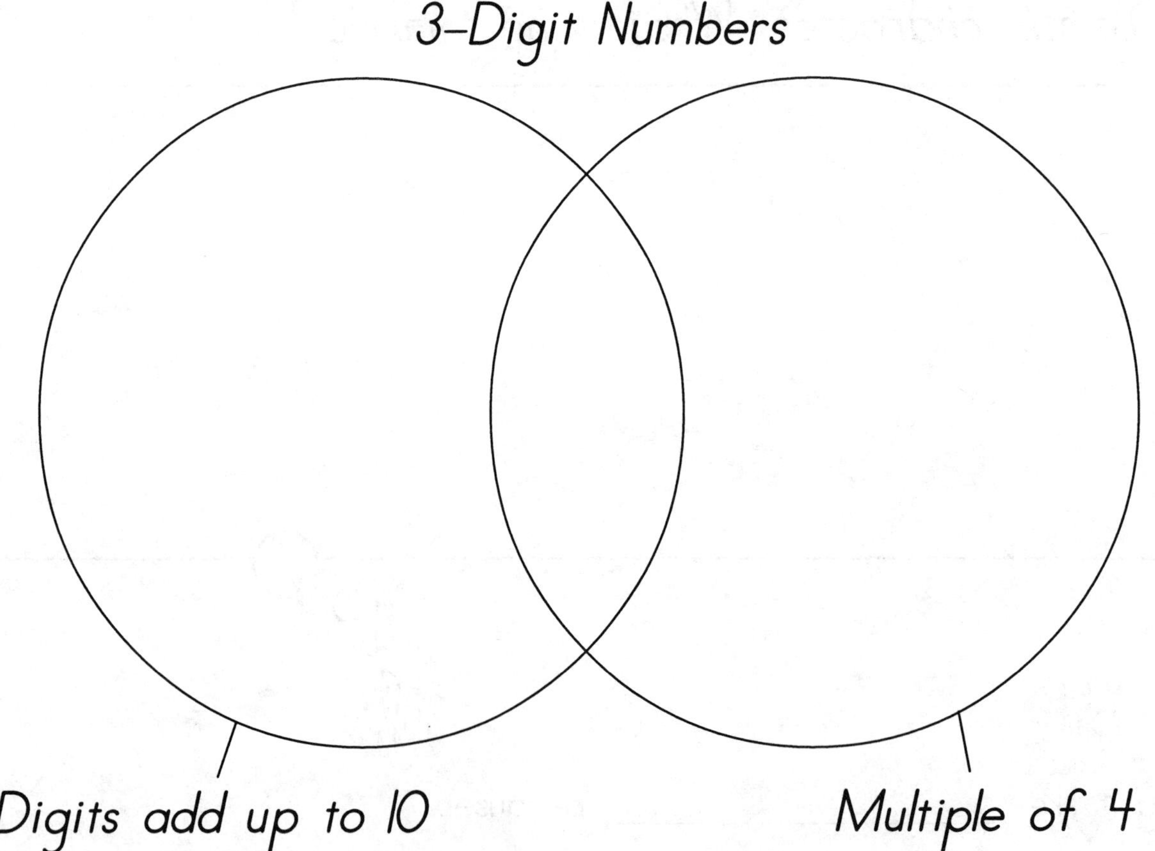

© ECS Learning Systems, Inc. All Rights Reserved.

Look at a map. Find a country that looks like a—

- plate

- person

- piece of furniture

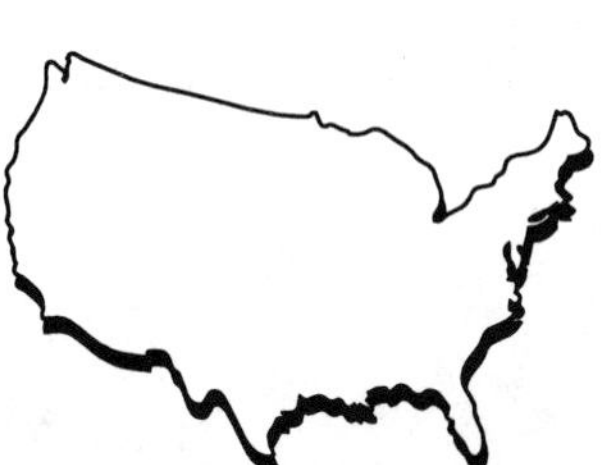

© ECS Learning Systems, Inc. All Rights Reserved.

3–minute list—

Animals that live in the desert...

Go!

© ECS Learning Systems, Inc. All Rights Reserved.

You have a basketball, chalk, and a bell. Invent a new game.

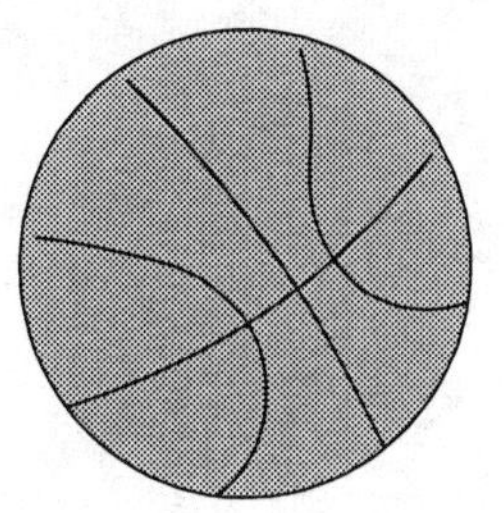

© ECS Learning Systems, Inc. All Rights Reserved.

Bell is to ring as ______________________ is to ______________________ .

Start with the word **harm**. Make new words by changing one letter at a time.

Example: harm → harp → carp

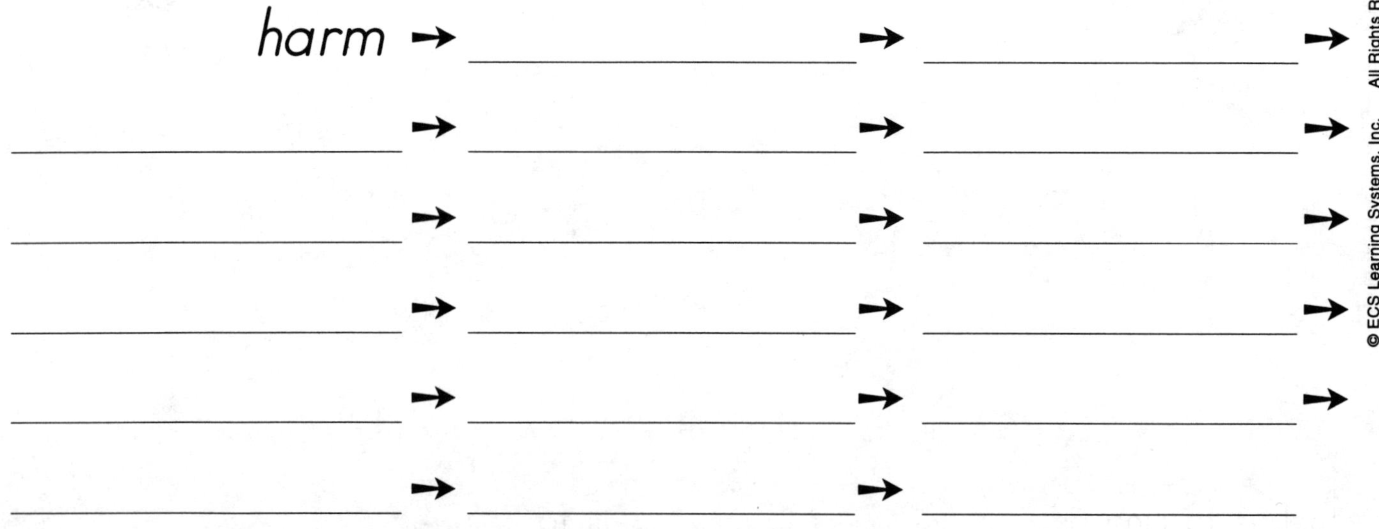

© ECS Learning Systems, Inc. All Rights Reserved.

If I lived on the moon—

Draw!

© ECS Learning Systems, Inc.   All Rights Reserved.

When I look at the moon...

Choose—Would you rather be

a cave

or

a mountain?

Why?

© ECS Learning Systems, Inc. All Rights Reserved.

How many ways can you roll a sum of 12 with 3 dice?

Example: 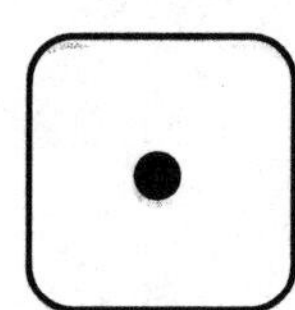 +  + 

Dice are to ______________________ as cards are to ______________________ .

© ECS Learning Systems, Inc. All Rights Reserved.

In the Winter

animals	plants

© ECS Learning Systems, Inc. All Rights Reserved.

The answer is **fossil**. Write some funny questions.

1. ____?

2. ____?

3. ____?

4. ____?

5. ____?

6. ____?

© ECS Learning Systems, Inc. All Rights Reserved.

A fossil is like ____________________ because...

Waves on a beach sound like...

© ECS Learning Systems, Inc. All Rights Reserved.

A happy hippopotamus would always—

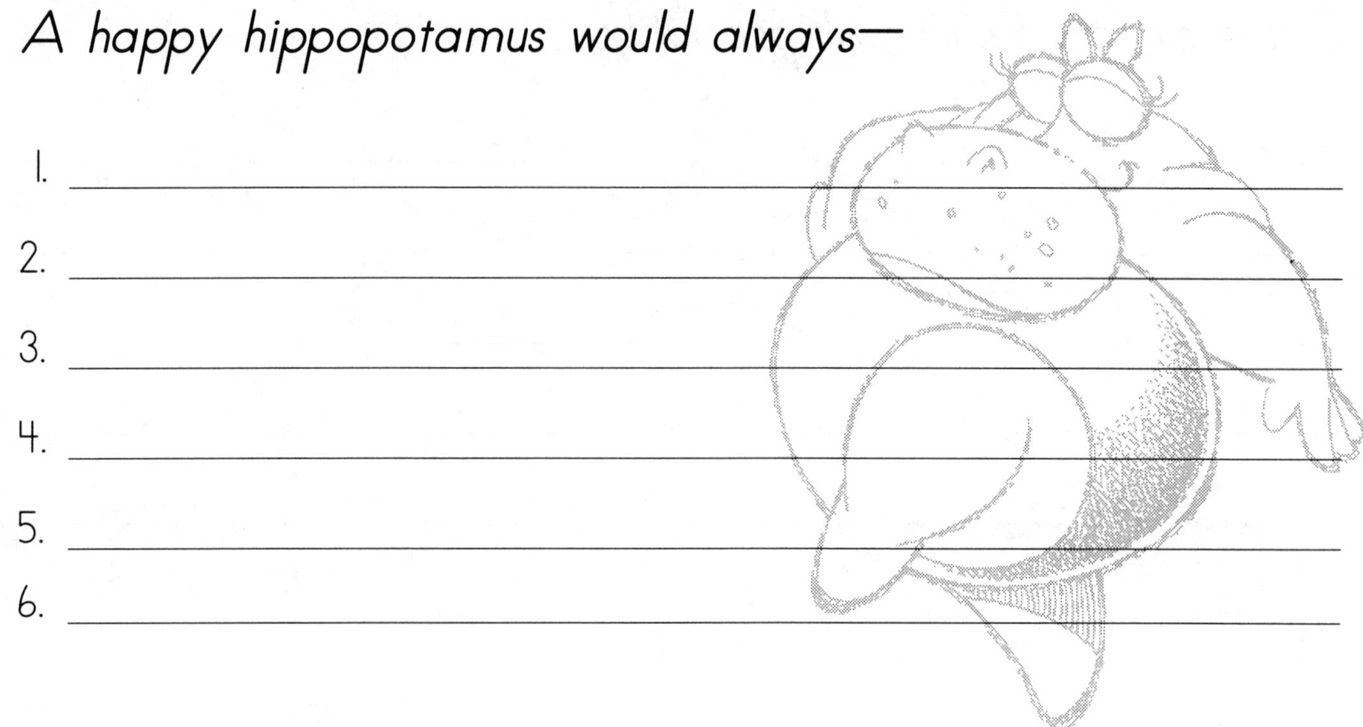

1. ______________________________

2. ______________________________

3. ______________________________

4. ______________________________

5. ______________________________

6. ______________________________

© ECS Learning Systems, Inc. All Rights Reserved.

Dancing is to ______________ as drawing is to ______________ .

Cities of the future will probably...

© ECS Learning Systems, Inc. All Rights Reserved.

Cities of the future—

Draw!

© ECS Learning Systems, Inc. All Rights Reserved.

Present is to ______________________ as future is to ______________________ .

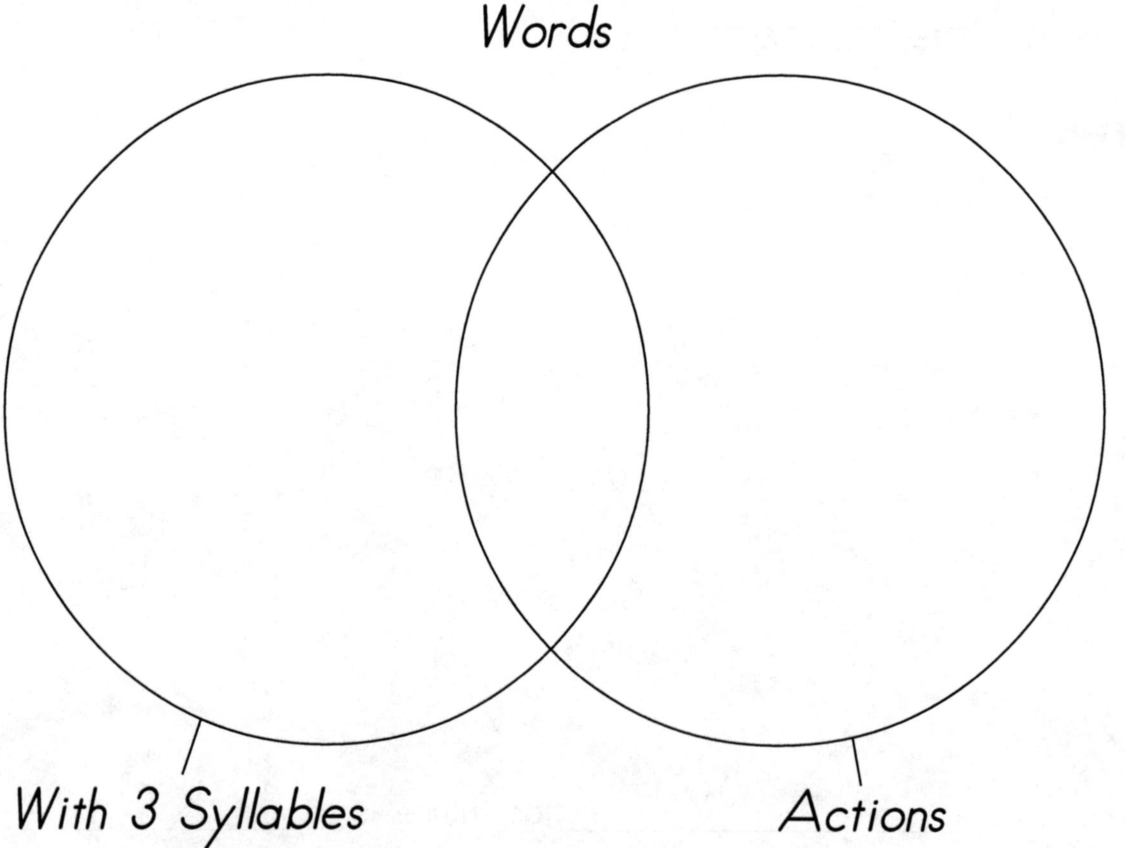

© ECS Learning Systems, Inc. All Rights Reserved.

*The **re** in rerun means again. How many **re** words do you know?*

Reruns on TV are like ____________________ because...

© ECS Learning Systems, Inc. All Rights Reserved.

Use the squiggle as part of an outerspace picture.

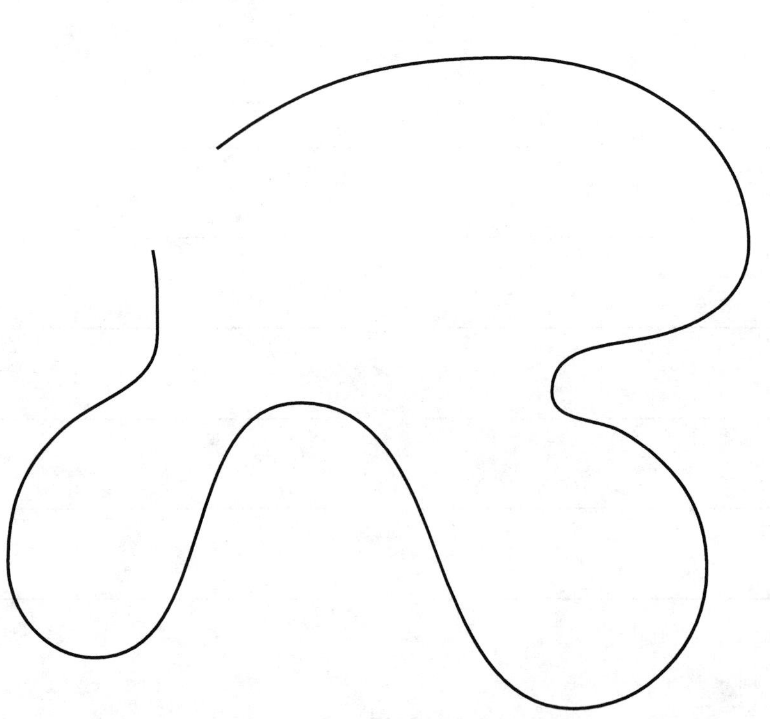

© ECS Learning Systems, Inc. All Rights Reserved.

How many ways can you roll a product of 24 with 3 dice?

Example:  x 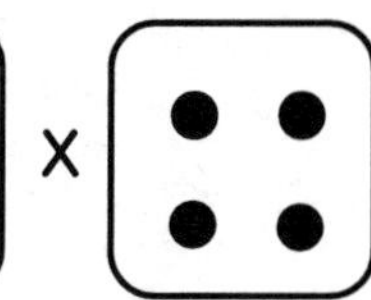 x 

© ECS Learning Systems, Inc. All Rights Reserved.

Multiplication is like ______________________ because...

You are an insect in the grass. What do you see?

Draw!

© ECS Learning Systems, Inc. All Rights Reserved.

3-minute list—

New uses for old newspaper...

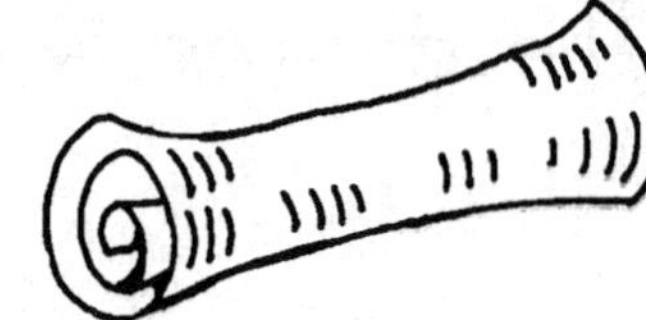

Go!

© ECS Learning Systems, Inc. All Rights Reserved.

*The answer is **Icicle Man.** Write some silly questions.*

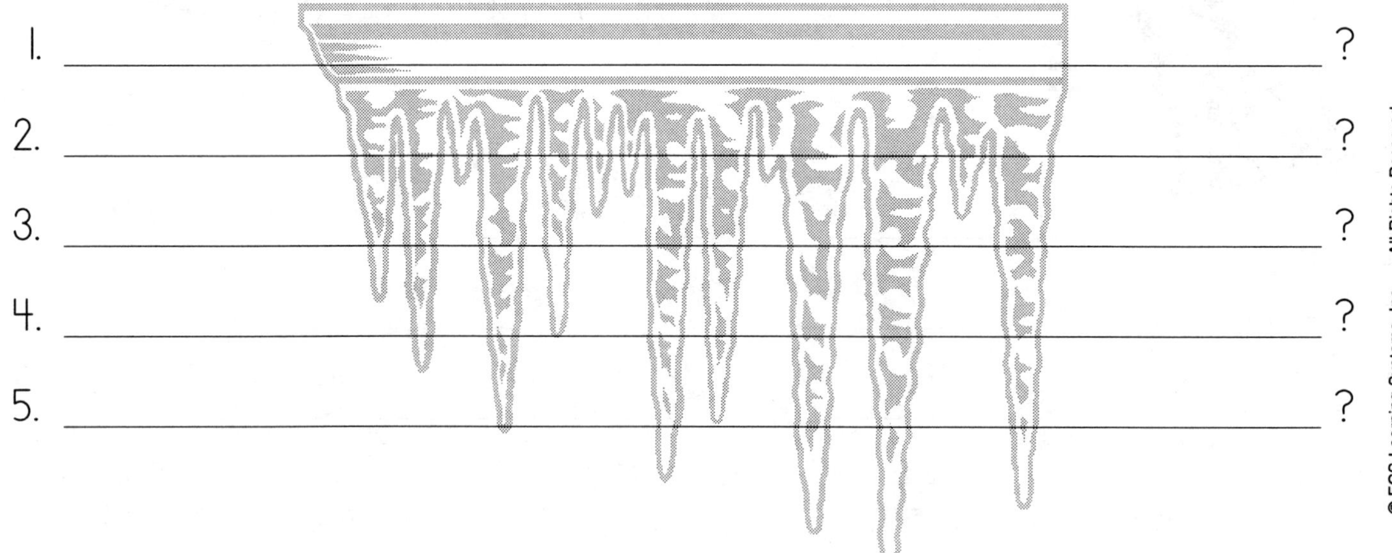

1. ______________________________ ?
2. ______________________________ ?
3. ______________________________ ?
4. ______________________________ ?
5. ______________________________ ?

© ECS Learning Systems, Inc. All Rights Reserved.

An icicle is like ____________________ because...

Communication

insects

birds

© ECS Learning Systems, Inc. All Rights Reserved.

If sadness had a shape and a color, it would look like this—

Draw!

Sadness is to ____________________ as happiness is to ____________________ .

© ECS Learning Systems, Inc. All Rights Reserved.

The answer is **104**. Write some problems.

☐ + ☐ = 104

☐ − ☐ = 104

☐ x ☐ = 104

☐ ÷ ☐ = 104

Can you think of others?

© ECS Learning Systems, Inc. All Rights Reserved.

When I hear the word ***danger****, I think about—*

Draw!

© ECS Learning Systems, Inc. All Rights Reserved.

Danger is to ____________________ as safety is to ____________________ .

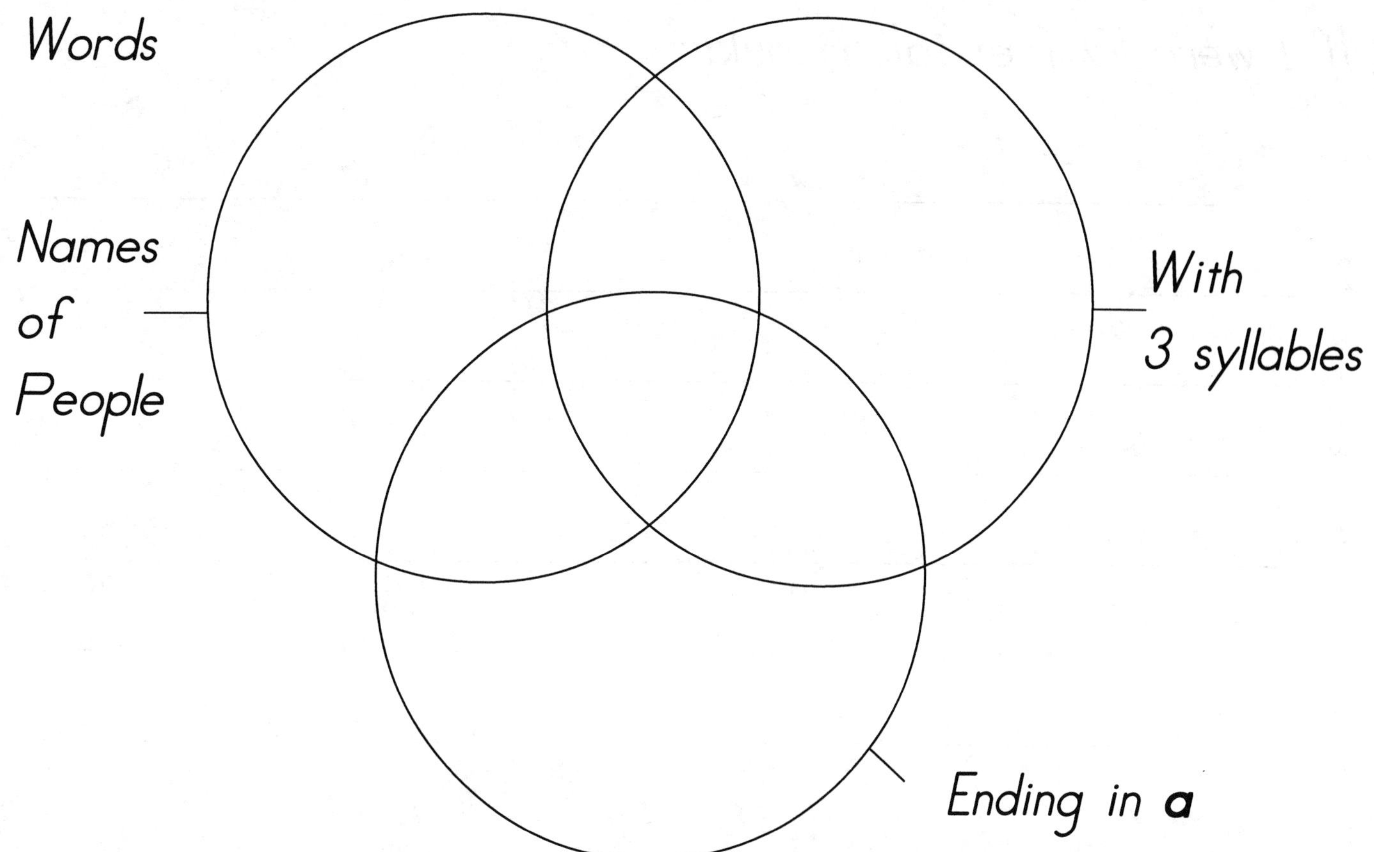

© ECS Learning Systems, Inc. All Rights Reserved.

If I were 10 feet tall, I could—

1. ____________________

2. ____________________

3. ____________________

4. ____________________

5. ____________________

6. ____________________

7. ____________________

© ECS Learning Systems, Inc. All Rights Reserved.

Wind + clouds =

© ECS Learning Systems, Inc. All Rights Reserved.

Write sentences that only have words beginning with ***t****.*

1. ______________________________

2. ______________________________

3. ______________________________

4. ______________________________

5. ______________________________

6. ______________________________

My favorite word is ______________ because...

© ECS Learning Systems, Inc. All Rights Reserved.

Morning sights and sounds—

© ECS Learning Systems, Inc. All Rights Reserved.

Morning is to ______________________ as evening is to ______________________ .

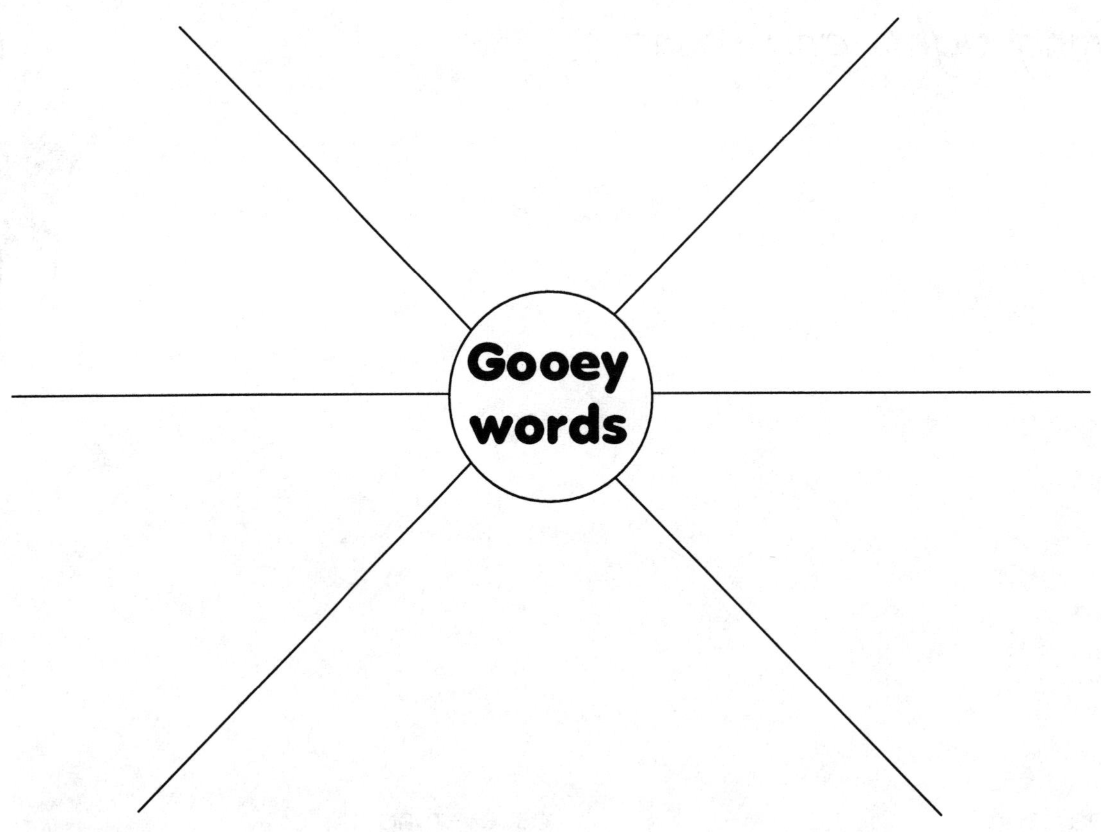

© ECS Learning Systems, Inc. All Rights Reserved.

Create a "gooey" treat.

Draw!

© ECS Learning Systems, Inc. All Rights Reserved.

Use the shape as part of an underwater picture.

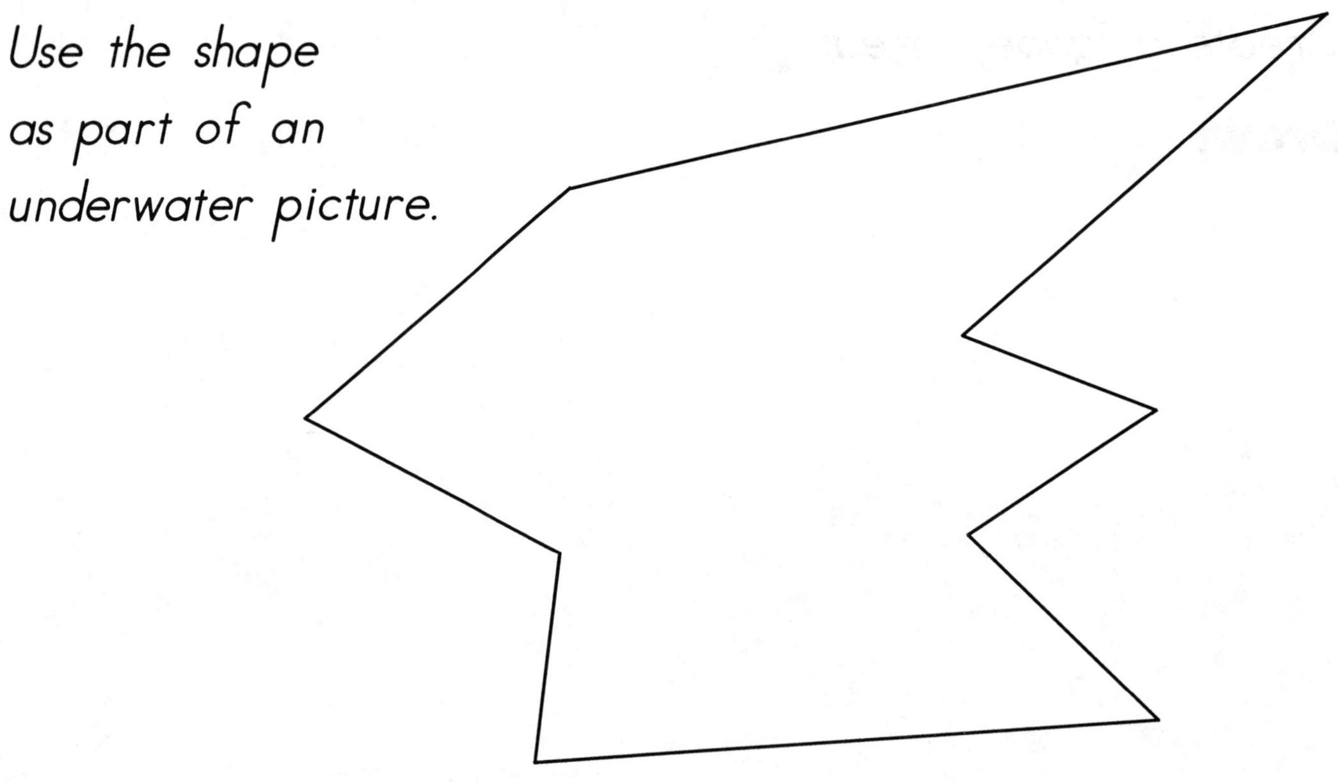

Under is to ______________________ as over is to ______________________ .

© ECS Learning Systems, Inc. All Rights Reserved.

3-minute list—

Common word pairs...

Example: bacon + eggs

© ECS Learning Systems, Inc. All Rights Reserved.

Pioneers

today	100 years ago

A pioneer is like ________________________ because...

© ECS Learning Systems, Inc. All Rights Reserved.

The best math trick I know...

© ECS Learning Systems, Inc. All Rights Reserved.

Rank 10 words that mean **big** from strongest to weakest.

Strongest ____________________

____

____

____

____

____

____

____

____

____________________ ***Weakest***

Weak is to ______________ as strong is to ______________ .

© ECS Learning Systems, Inc. All Rights Reserved.

Invent 3 new ways to say "Good morning."

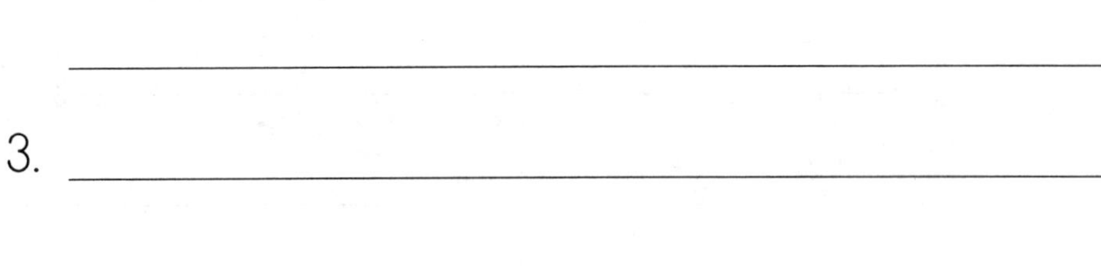

1.

2.

3.

© ECS Learning Systems, Inc. All Rights Reserved.

An **ode** is a poem that praises someone or something. Write an "Ode to an Insect."

© ECS Learning Systems, Inc. All Rights Reserved.

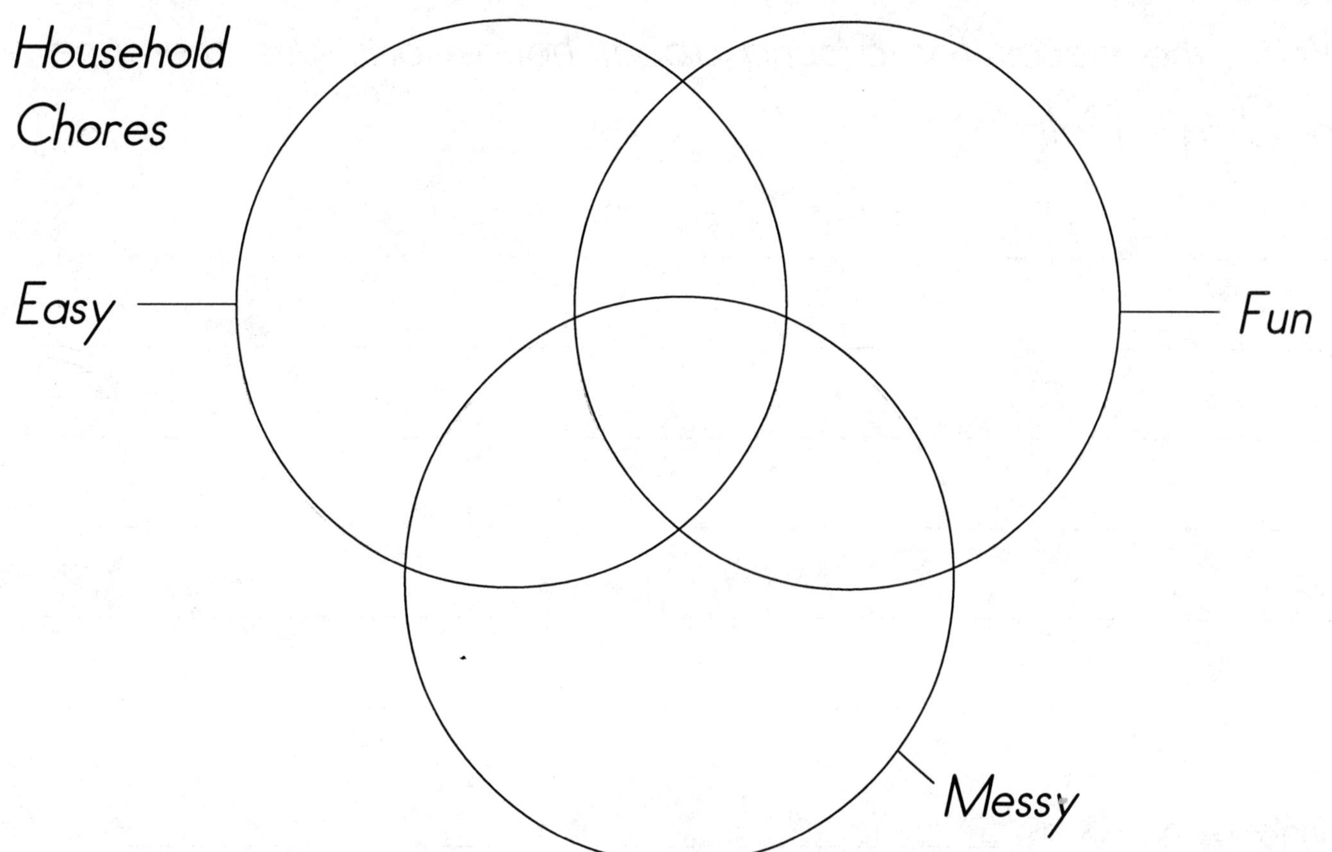

© ECS Learning Systems, Inc. All Rights Reserved.

Write the words for a song about housework. Use the tune to "Jingle Bells."

____

____

____

____

____

____

Jingle is to bells as ____________________ is to ____________________ .

© ECS Learning Systems, Inc. All Rights Reserved.

The answer is **210**. Write some problems.

$\square + \square = 210$

$\square - \square = 210$

$\square \times \square = 210$

$\square \div \square = 210$

© ECS Learning Systems, Inc. All Rights Reserved.

I know it's going to be a great day when—

1. ________________________________
2. ________________________________
3. ________________________________
4. ________________________________
5. ________________________________
6. ________________________________
7. ________________________________

© ECS Learning Systems, Inc. All Rights Reserved.

I know it's going to be a terrible day when—

1. __________
2. __________
3. __________
4. __________
5. __________
6. __________
7. __________

© ECS Learning Systems, Inc. All Rights Reserved.

If I were only 6 inches tall—

Draw!

© ECS Learning Systems, Inc. All Rights Reserved.

Tall is to ______________________ as short is to ______________________ .

Raindrops + music =

Music is like ______________________ because...

© ECS Learning Systems, Inc. All Rights Reserved.

Choose—Would you rather be

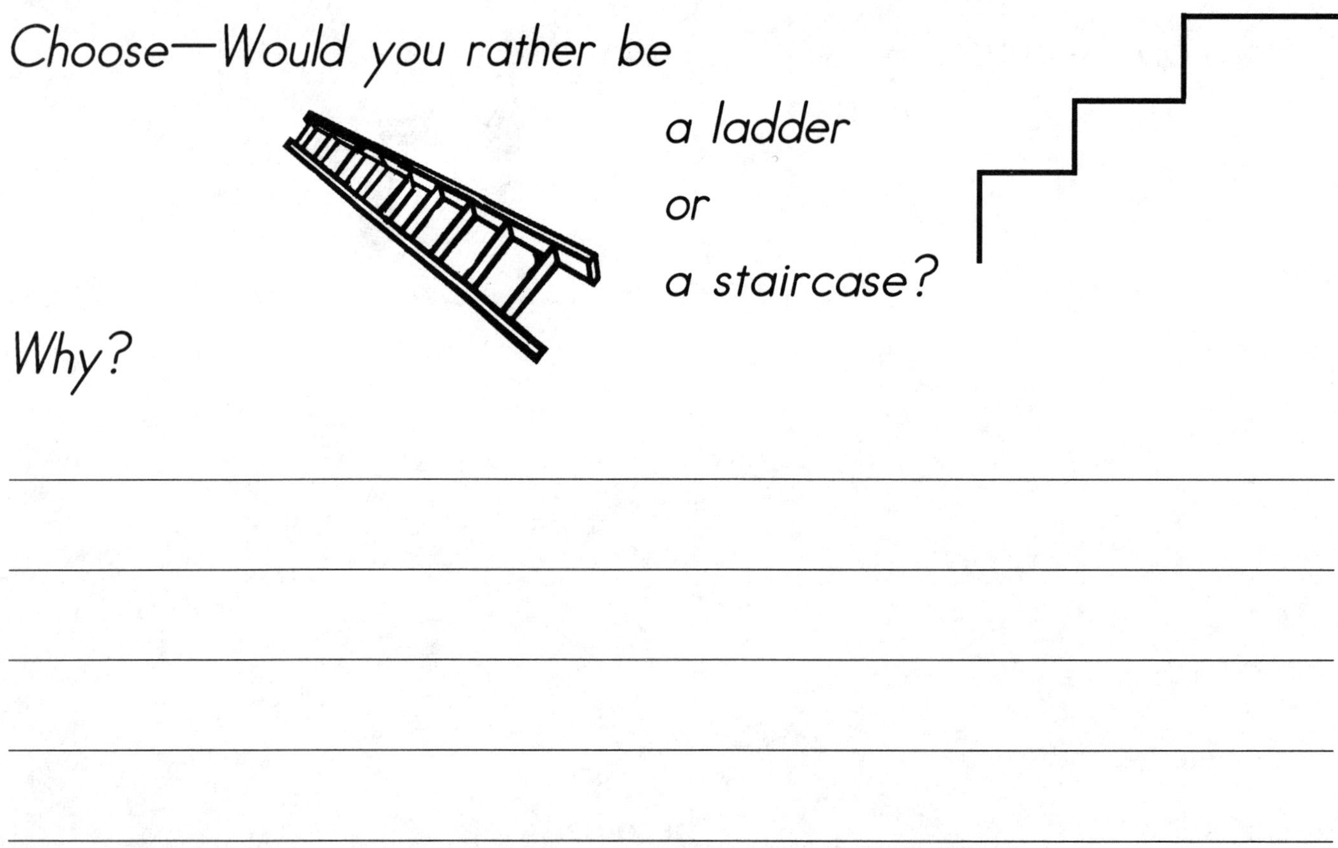

a ladder

or

a staircase?

Why?

© ECS Learning Systems, Inc. All Rights Reserved.

When I hear the word ***surprise,*** *I think about—*

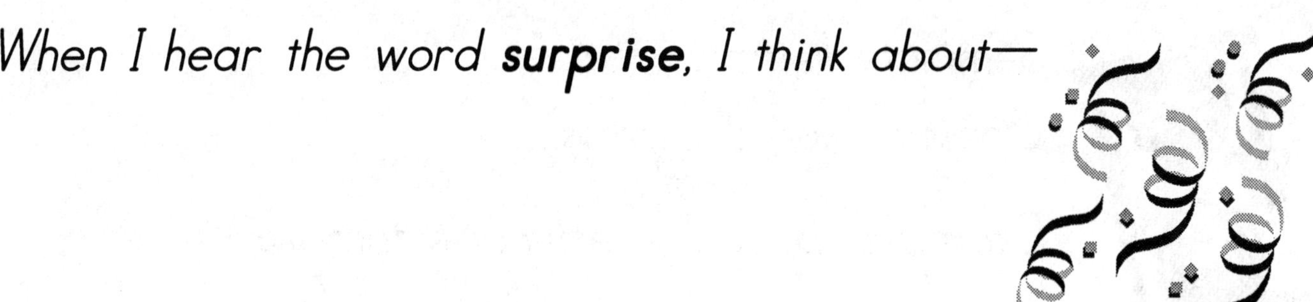

© ECS Learning Systems, Inc. All Rights Reserved.

A surprise is like ______________________ because...

3–minute list—

Common word triplets...

Example: bacon + lettuce + tomato

© ECS Learning Systems, Inc. All Rights Reserved.

If I had a twin...

Early in the morning, things outside seem to—

The morning sun is like ____________________ because...

© ECS Learning Systems, Inc. All Rights Reserved.

Start with the word **flow**. Make new words by changing one letter at a time.

Example: flow → slow → slaw

flow → ________ → ________ →

________ → ________ → ________ →

________ → ________ → ________ →

________ → ________ → ________ →

________ → ________ → ________ →

________ → ________ → ________

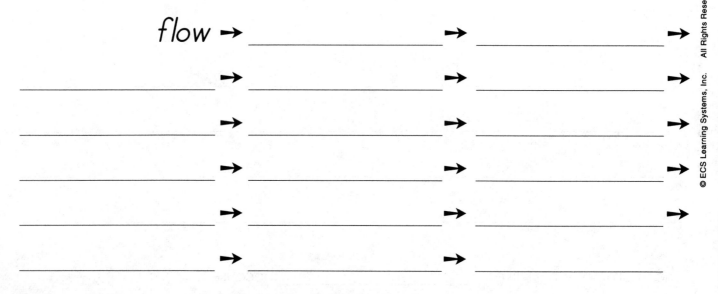

© ECS Learning Systems, Inc. All Rights Reserved.

Write sentences that only have words beginning with ***m****.*

1. ______________________________

2. ______________________________

3. ______________________________

4. ______________________________

5. ______________________________

6. ______________________________

© ECS Learning Systems, Inc. All Rights Reserved.

Many muddy monkeys might...

Rank 10 words that mean **nice** from strongest to weakest.

Strongest ____________________

____

____

____

____

____

____

____

____

____________________ Weakest

© ECS Learning Systems, Inc. All Rights Reserved.

Use the squiggle as part of a garden picture.

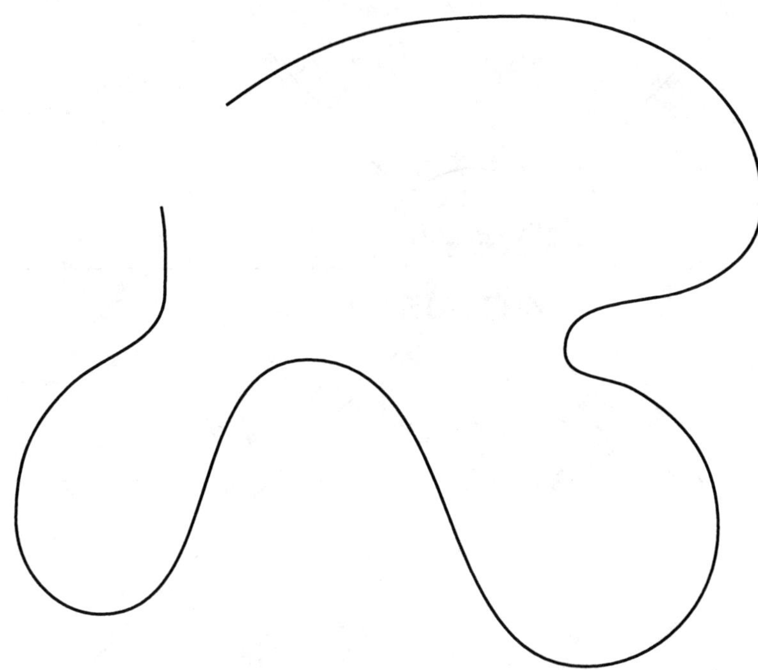

A garden is like...

© ECS Learning Systems, Inc. All Rights Reserved.

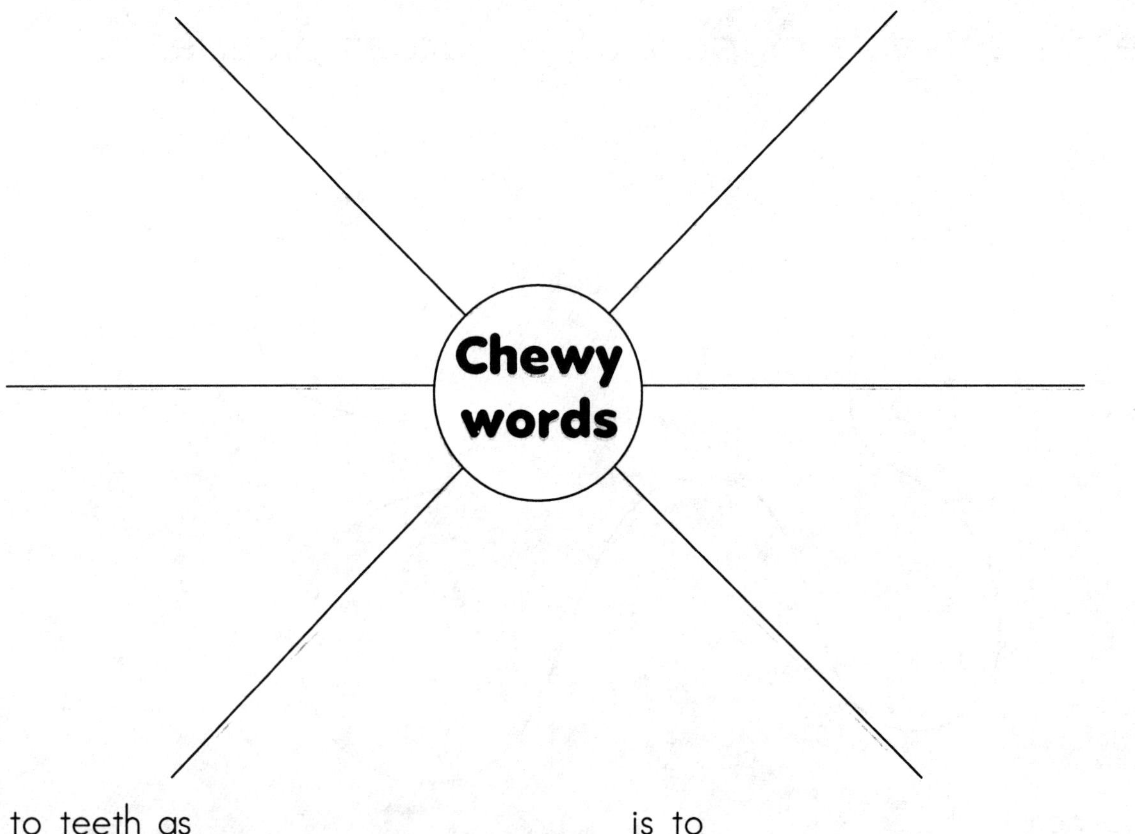

Chew is to teeth as ______________________ is to ______________________ .

© ECS Learning Systems, Inc. All Rights Reserved.

A Good Friend

would always...

would never...

© ECS Learning Systems, Inc. All Rights Reserved.

If I could travel 100 years into the future—

Draw!

Past is to ______________________ as future is to ______________________ .

© ECS Learning Systems, Inc. All Rights Reserved.

You have a ruler, a rope, and a blanket. What could you make?

© ECS Learning Systems, Inc. All Rights Reserved.

The answer is **constellation**. What are some questions?

1. ____ ?

2. ____ ?

3. ____ ?

4. ____ ?

5. ____ ?

© ECS Learning Systems, Inc. All Rights Reserved.

Choose—Would you rather be

a pet dragon

or

a pet gorilla?

Why?

____

____

____

If a dragon visited my home...

© ECS Learning Systems, Inc. All Rights Reserved.

Create a bumper sticker message about your favorite sport.

Baseball is to ____________________ as ice hockey is to ____________________ .

© ECS Learning Systems, Inc. All Rights Reserved.

3-minute list—

Cities that have 2-word names...

Go!

© ECS Learning Systems, Inc. All Rights Reserved.

How many ways can you roll a product of 18 with 3 dice?

Example: 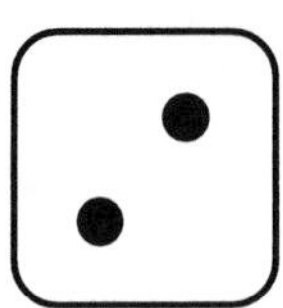 x 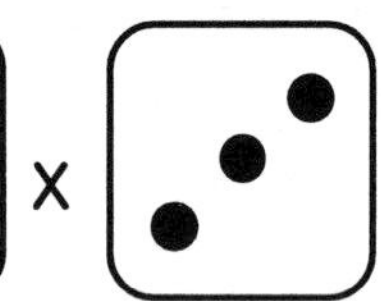 x 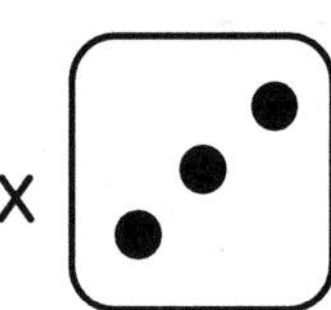

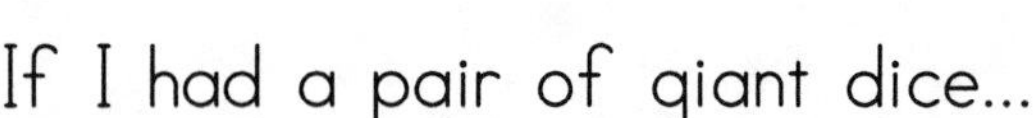

© ECS Learning Systems, Inc. All Rights Reserved.

If I lived high in a tree...

© ECS Learning Systems, Inc. All Rights Reserved.

Use these lines as part of a sports picture.

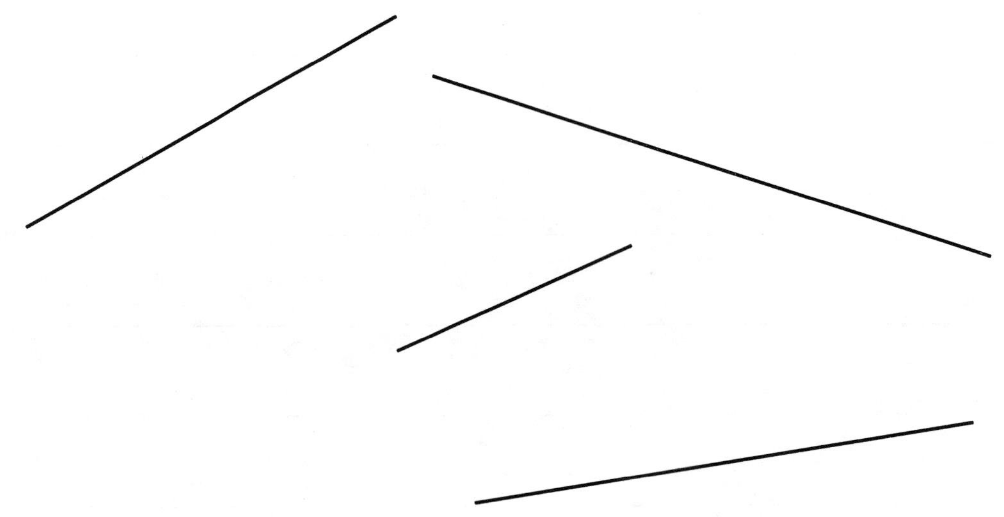

© ECS Learning Systems, Inc. All Rights Reserved.

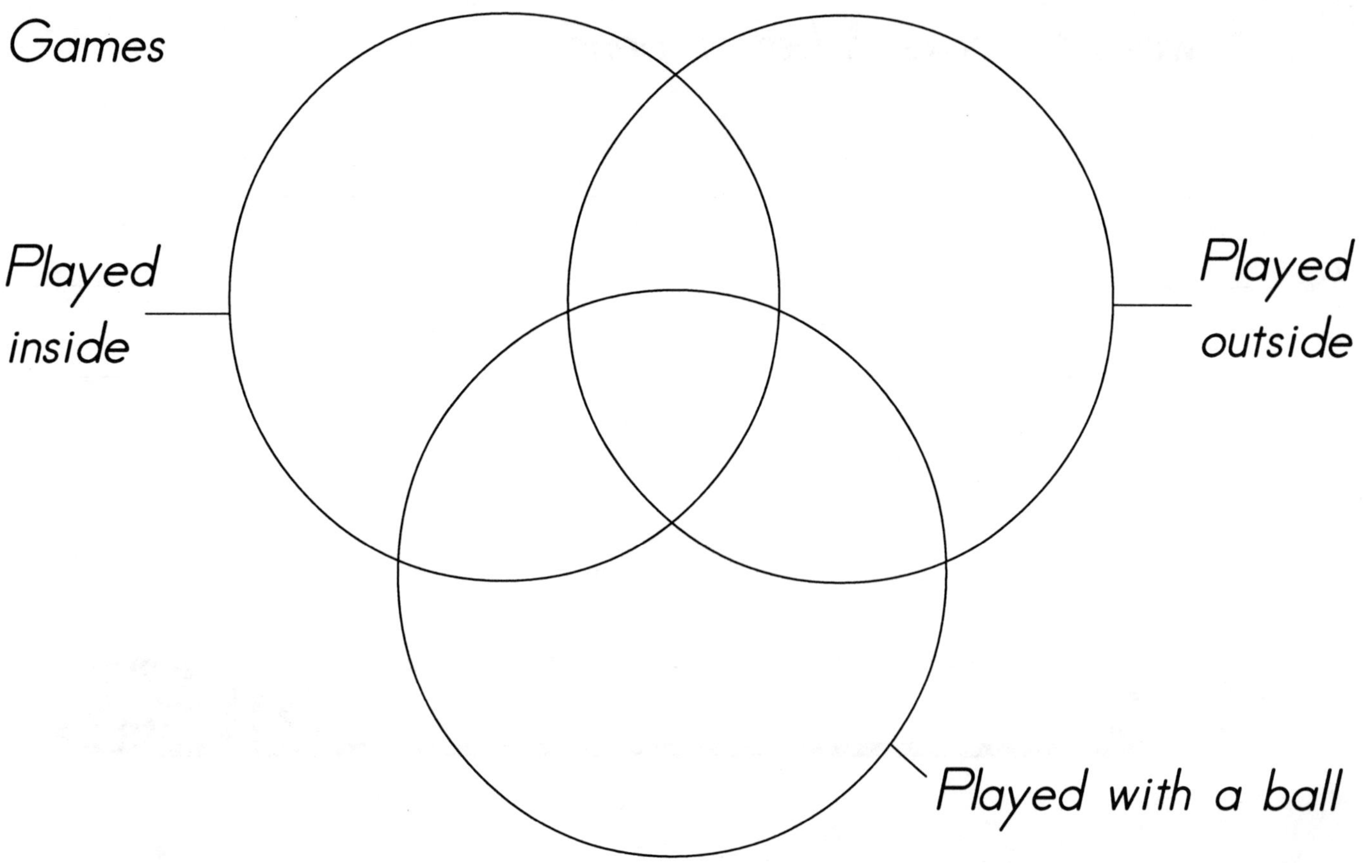

© ECS Learning Systems, Inc. All Rights Reserved.

List 5 ways to make a better pencil.

1. ______________________________

2. ______________________________

3. ______________________________

4. ______________________________

5. ______________________________

© ECS Learning Systems, Inc. All Rights Reserved.

Draw a picture of a "better pencil."

© ECS Learning Systems, Inc. All Rights Reserved.

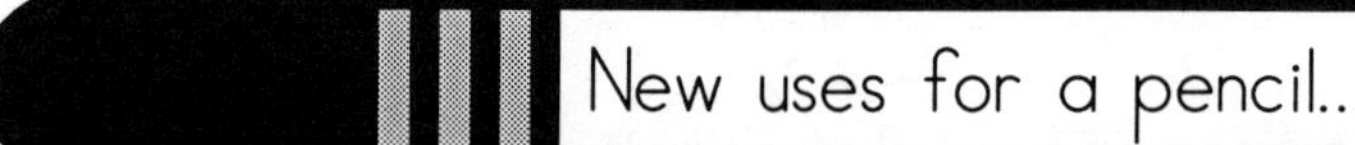

Start with the word **give**. Make new words by changing one letter at a time.

Example: give → live → line

give → ____________ → ____________ →

____________ → ____________ → ____________ →

____________ → ____________ → ____________ →

____________ → ____________ → ____________ →

____________ → ____________ → ____________ →

____________ → ____________ → ____________

© ECS Learning Systems, Inc. All Rights Reserved.

Write sentences that only have words beginning with ***g***.

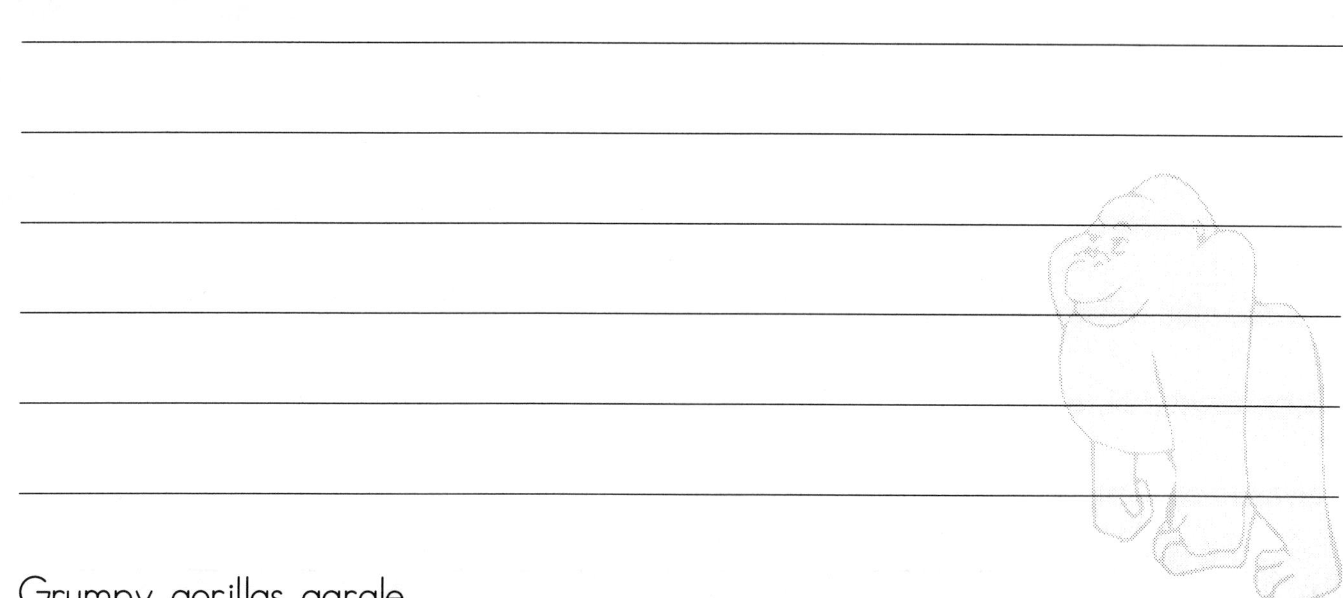

Grumpy gorillas gargle...

© ECS Learning Systems, Inc. All Rights Reserved.

The ***tri*** *in tricycle means three. How many* ***tri*** *words can you list?*

© ECS Learning Systems, Inc. All Rights Reserved.

Look at a map. Find a country that looks like—

- an animal

- a punctuation mark

- a sea monster

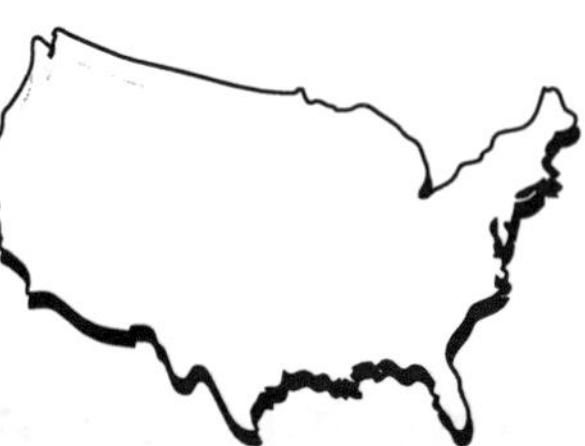

If I could visit any country...

© ECS Learning Systems, Inc. All Rights Reserved.

How many ways can you roll an answer of 10 with 3 dice?

Example: [2] x [6] − [2]

Solving math problems is better than...

© ECS Learning Systems, Inc. All Rights Reserved.

3-minute list—

Things that should glow in the dark...

Go!

© ECS Learning Systems, Inc. All Rights Reserved.

You have a stone, a twig, and a glove. Invent a new game.

© ECS Learning Systems, Inc. All Rights Reserved.

A dancing dinosaur might—

© ECS Learning Systems, Inc. All Rights Reserved.

What kind of dance does a dinosaur do?

Rank 10 words that mean **pretty** from strongest to weakest.

Strongest ______________________

____

____

____

____

____

____

____

____

______________________ Weakest

© ECS Learning Systems, Inc. All Rights Reserved.

Living near the Ocean

benefits	problems

Riding a wave is like...

© ECS Learning Systems, Inc. All Rights Reserved.

A traffic jam looks like...

© ECS Learning Systems, Inc. All Rights Reserved.

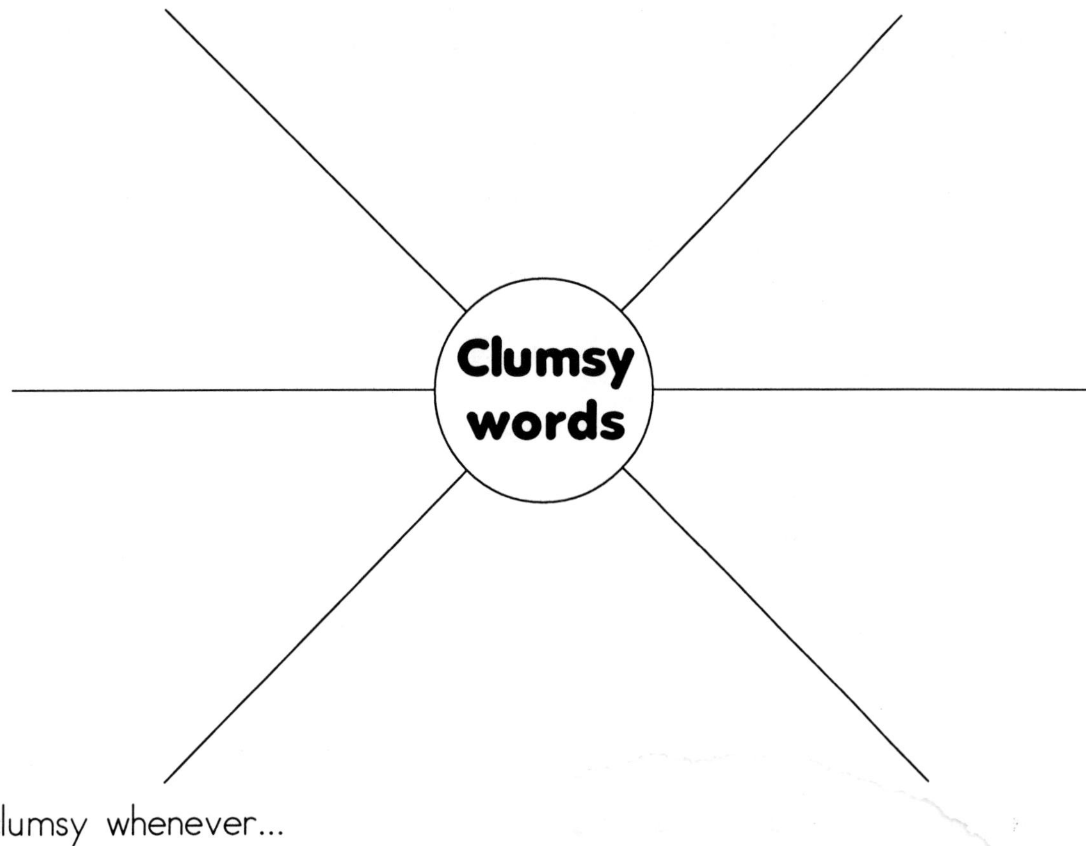

I feel clumsy whenever...

© ECS Learning Systems, Inc. All Rights Reserved.

If I could travel 100 years into the past...

Draw!

© ECS Learning Systems, Inc. All Rights Reserved.

Long, long ago in a faraway place...

*The answer is **pumpkin**. What are some questions?*

1. ____?

2. ____?

3. ____?

4. ____?

5. ____?

© ECS Learning Systems, Inc. All Rights Reserved.

If jealousy had a shape and a color, it would look like this—

Draw!

Jealousy is like ________________________ because...

© ECS Learning Systems, Inc. All Rights Reserved.

Sunshine + dewdrops =

© ECS Learning Systems, Inc. All Rights Reserved.

3-minute list—

Famous people who have your first name...

Go!

© ECS Learning Systems, Inc. All Rights Reserved.

If people had two pairs of eyes...

© ECS Learning Systems, Inc. All Rights Reserved.

So Many Fun Ways to Learn . . .

Titles from the Home Study Collection™

Activity Books: These books teach what children need to know for school success. They include challenging and interesting lessons, learning activities for family involvement, and answer keys.

Reading and More: Grade 1, Grade 2, Grade 3, Grade 4, Grade 5, Grade 6 $4.95 ea.
Language Arts and More: Grade 1, Grade 2, Grade 3, Grade 4, Grade 5, Grade 6 $4.95 ea.
Math and More: Grade 1, Grade 2, Grade 3, Grade 4, Grade 5, Grade 6 $4.95 ea.

The Little Red Writing Book: Book 1 (ages 6-7), Book 2 (ages 8-9), & Book 3 (ages 10-12) $8.95 ea.
The Bright Blue Thinking Book: Book 1 (ages 6-7), Book 2 (ages 8-9), & Book 3 (ages 10-12) $8.95 ea.

Parent Resource: Answers your parenting questions.

Parent Talk, Ages 2-5 $14.95

These books are available through your local book/school supply stores.

Published by
ECS Learning Systems, Inc.
San Antonio, TX 78279-1437